Praise fo
The Astrological Elements Book 1

"I thoroughly enjoyed this book. I gained new perspective on Mercury and Venus in the context of the Sun, as well as on singletons versus missing elements. Lots to ruminate on here, and I expect to return to it and the companion volume (Earth and Air) for additional insights."
— QuetzalBacon

"Ms. Costello has a love of literature and etymology that makes her lectures an erudite experience. She quotes poets and writers and has a strong appreciation for Western literary tradition, but there is something else at work here - she is familiar with the imaginative realms, with astrology as a language of Soul and Spirit, and her teaching unabashedly conveys this view. Her thoughts will serve to fuel the imagination of any who may feel stuck in too literal a view of how the elements act in a human life."
— Mary Plumb

"Yes, the book is quite thorough in its analysis of the water and fire elements. Yes, there is a lot of information to digest and yes, I learned a lot. But the absolute value of this book for me was the shift in perspective on how I consider the elements."
— Fabienne Lopez

WATER & FIRE

The Astrological Elements

Part One

Also by Darby Costello

The Astrological Moon

Earth and Air:
The Astrological Elements Part Two

Pockets Astrology
with Lindsay Radermacher

WATER & FIRE
THE ASTROLOGICAL ELEMENTS

PART ONE

DARBY COSTELLO

RAVEN
DREAMS
PRESS

Raven Dreams Press
Portland, OR

Published 2019 by Raven Dreams Press
2621 NE 7th Ave #301
Portland, OR 97212
www.ravendreamspress.com

First published 1999 by The Centre for
Psychological Astrology Press.

E-book published by the Centre for
Psychological Astrology Press, 2013.
E-book republished by Raven Dreams Press, 2019.

WATER AND FIRE

ISBN 978-1-7326504-1-1
LCCN 2019930726

British Library Cataloguing-in-Publication
Data. The original catalogue record for this book
is available from the British Library.

TABLE OF CONTENTS

ACKNOWLEDGEMENTS

Several of my friends read the text as it was progressing through its stages: Bridget Belgrave, Elisa Banks, Bridget and Misha Norland each gave me their thoughts and feelings, which delighted and enlightened me. The students of the CPA gave me the exciting dialogues which formed the base of this work.

Stephen gave the evolving text the generosity of his full attention for weeks. And Liz made it all possible.

PART ONE

WATER,

The Womb, Death, and the Dream

This seminar was given on 28 January, 1996 at Regents College, London as part of the Winter Term of the seminar programme of the Centre for Psychological Astrology.

INTRODUCTION

L et us start this day in the realm of water with the image of a circle. As astrologers we naturally have circles at the centre of all of our discussions, but with today's theme a circle has even more resonance than usual. This is because it says something essential about the nature of water and its natural tendency to return to itself – to self-contain. Left to its own devices it would always and everywhere end up encircling itself. What stops it is gravity – gravity pulls it downwards. When gravity does not interfere, water tends to create a circle. Its nature is to self-enclose.

Seeking unity

We could say that water is always seeking unity – every drop of water on the earth is always heading for the sea. Even in our city lives we can see that, if we look closely enough. Turn on the tap and watch the water run down the hole into the pipes to begin its long journey to the sea. On reaching the sea it merges into this greater body of water. The clouds above us, which produce the rain that waters the earth, come from the water that evaporates from the surface of the sea. The rain pours down, and becomes ground water which feeds underground streams, which then get to the tap which we open to receive the water we need. Water is everywhere returning to itself. Water is about seeking unity.

We see in water's unity-seeking nature our own longing for oneness with something beyond ourselves. The wisdom of water is connected to the search for compassion that, in turn, leads us to know the secret unity of all creation. As all water heads for the sea, all creation heads for another kind of sea – we might say a cosmic sea, out of which everything is born again.

The very nature of water is to penetrate and dissolve, unify and absorb. In itself it generates religious feelings, in the sense that it can bring you experiences of eternity. A day fishing in the rain, if you like that sort of thing, can bring eternal peace to one's soul – for a time! We go to seas, oceans and lakes to relax, to loosen up and to dissolve our knots, both physical and psychological. For those of us who love holidays by the sea, lakes or rivers, it is this dissolving effect of water that draws us again and again. Often, even a day by the sea can seem to loosen the grip of the most tangled problems, or at least release the pressure so that we can think about them properly. We return to the womb of the sea, our waters "remember" their source; we are cut loose from our entanglements, our workaday selves die, and we are free to dream. When we return to our everyday lives, we are born anew. It feels that way, for a period of time.

And when water has had its benefic effect, we feel something close to a religious feeling. We loosen our boundaries and feel more of a sense of oneness with life – we become more generous, more open. There is a feeling of absolution in this. We think, "I could die today, and it would be well." Many of us feel, or hope, that death will be a dissolving of our problematic sense of separation. When we long for the sea, we are longing for a release from the tension of spirit incarnated into matter. It is thought to be both a longing for the womb, and a longing for death, but this death we long for is ego death – death of that which separates us from what we instinctively feel to be our source. We dream of this oneness with what some of us call God – though it is disguised in all sorts of wrappings.

We can think of water representing the desire to return to the womb, that watery place where every single part of us is in constant touch with something that is, mostly, physically benevolent. There, we were totally in touch with our environment, one with it. We have those tiny little hairs on our body and in the womb, and they are constantly waving and constantly massage the foetus as it grows. Psychologically, from water's perspective, it reminds us of the source of our desire for God, when God is conceived of as oneness, security, safety. Out of the water, we are separate and alone, and one way or another we long to get back to that feeling of oneness. Religions are built partly on this longing. We are born out of that water into a world that is immediately harsher unless, presumably, we are born into a water birth.

Meandering and reflecting

Let me give you some ideas and images from a book titled *Water and Sexuality* by Michel Odent. We looked at some of his images and ideas when we were doing the Moon seminars, if you remember. The title is slightly misleading in that it is not about sexuality in the sense that we Neptune in Libra and Scorpio people might think of it, but it is about birth, specifically about water birth. Michel Odent is one of the water birth kings, so to speak. In this book he promotes the idea that we have evolved from sea animals, and he tells us that watching babies who are born in water is absolute proof of this. In the course of his proving his point, he gives some wonderful insights into the element of water. Let me quote him here: "Water always takes a meandering course. It never goes straight, unless it is forced to through a tunnel or tube, but its nature when it starts out high, going to the sea, is to take a meandering course."

Water adapts to its environment, moving round things, over things, through things if it has to. If it is stopped by an obstacle, it will wear it away, given time. Its action is to smooth anything that it touches, given time, and eventually to wear it away, absorb it into itself, dissolve it. And listen to this: "Even within meanders there are secondary currents with a circular sort of action, fascinating in their complexity. The meeting of two such currents can cause a spiraling movement. The loops become so pronounced that a flood can cause them to be by passed and left as back-waters...Water has a constant tendency to re-create a sphere...a raindrop is a sphere stretched by gravity." And so is a tear. Think of the intimacy of water – the intimacy that people crave, and the fear of intimacy and its attendant sense of loss.

We can understand astrological water as that which indi-cates the underlying longing to find that watery womb again. We can imagine that planets in water are always about the longing for unity. Cancer, Scorpio and Pisces have different images of this unity and different ways of doing it, but that's what they are seeking. The source of the longing for unity can be seen, from this perspective, as the memory of womb time. Now, this longing for unity implies separation, for why would you seek what you feel you already have? And so issues of separation, abandonment and neglect are part of any water story. We discover through time that nothing will let you be one with it for any length of time, not a person, not a subject, not an idea, not a chair, not a period of sleep, not food, not sex – nothing. So, because it is constantly seeking oneness, it is prone to disillusionment, is water. Wher-ever it is, whatever planets are in it, water's aim is to penetrate, to permeate and to dissolve. To dissolve itself and to dissolve the other object.

Audience: Which is where sex comes in. Sex is about merging and union, penetration and dissolving, separation, generation and birth. In your Moon seminar you said water was about re-flection. Sex and reflection? If we reflected more, I imagine we would have less sex.

Darby: This may be true, although youth is not generally asso-ciated with reflection. Youth is when the biological imperative to reproduce ourselves dominates, and reflection is hard then. Reflection comes out of experience. We develop the power of reflection after spending some time in messy unreflective living. Water draws us into experience and that experience is life, and it is only through living fully that we have any hope of achieving wisdom. Water experiences generate life in all its messiness, and this becomes the food for reflection that leads to wisdom. It looks like we need one and then the other to complete the circle.

And what about the sort of experiences that water constellates? The sea can overwhelm us – we can drown. We can become so immersed in water that we cannot see, cannot breathe. We can be crushed by water, wiped out, all consciousness drowned out. Water can suffocate us, render us helpless, toss us about in its relentless tumult until there is nothing left of us. Water can kill us too. We can become victims of water – lost and hopeless and overcome by its all-pervading, all penetrating power. We can be rained out, washed out, sapped of all energy, turned into mush, nothing but a piece of flotsam washed up on the shore. This is also water's effect.

Now for the structure of the day: I shall carry on speaking about water in general. After that we shall move on to the water signs, Cancer, Scorpio and Pisces. We'll look at the houses associated with water – the 4th, 8th and 12th – as we go along. I have brought a chart that I hope will interest you. It is very watery and will tell us more about the water signs and houses. As you all probably know, Mercury is retrograde today. If it doesn't play too many tricks, we'll get to progressions and transits and a few other things. Let's see how far we get!

LEVELS OF WATER

Terrestrial water

The *Encyclopedia Britannica* tells us that water is "a chemical compound of hydrogen and oxygen, having the formula H2O, [and] is one of the most abundant, widely distributed, and essential substances on earth." Water occurs in solid states as ice or snow, in liquid state as water, and in gaseous states as steam or vapour. Snow is thought to be its purest form, with rain a close second, although as my *Britannica* was published in 1970, this may no longer be considered true. There is also something called "heavy water", but it is derived from natural water.

Water for humans

Using water has always involved a lot of work, and also a lot of consciousness. We have always had to deal with the fact that water contains organisms that are not safe for our species. In many parts of the world, water-borne diseases are still a huge problem.

In the industralised parts of the world today, we have an unusual relationship to water, as we do to nature in general. Having developed ways of purifying it in large quantities and piping it straight into our private homes, we have lost consciousness of how much thought and care we must have around water. The water that arrives through our taps is relatively safe, clear and palatable, the move to bottled water notwithstanding.

While preparing this seminar I wrote a note to myself: "We must know how to purify the waters described in our charts.

Otherwise distortion, pollution, projection, illness, bad smells, whirlpools with attendant dead creatures keep our lives in a constant sluggish, tormented mess." I read this to a Pisces who is not so afraid of the mess of life, and he said, "Well, I don't know about purifying all the water – sounds a bit sterile to me. I don't think there's much life in purified water."

Audience: Purifying the water sounds very much a Uranian approach.

Darby: Yes, I suppose it does, especially when they use technology to do it. Sunlight naturally purifies moving water. Artificial purification, too much interfering with water, can result in a loss of vitality, creativity, life. But on the other hand, you can also sink in the sluggishness. However, you also need stagnant pools, because that's where new life forms grow in all their multiplicity.

Human beings are vulnerable to diseases that thrive in swamps and rainforests, but then these organisms which cause harm to us may be connected to organisms that are essential to us. Water carries all kinds of life forms. Some of these we need as part of our lives, in ways we understand. Some are needed by the wider ecological system but might harm us if we go too close. With water, if you leave it alone it will generate all sorts of life, some of it dangerous to us, some of it essential. Try to clean it up and you might destroy its creative capacity. Dealing with water requires wisdom. Wisdom and water.

Audience: There is an excellent poem by John Donne about that, called "Change":

> Waters stincke soone, if in one place they bide,
> And in the vast sea are more putrifi'd:
> But when they kisse one banke, and leaving this
> Never looke backe, but the next banke doe kisse,

Then are they purest: Change is the nursery
Of musicke, joy, life, and eternity.

Darby: That is lovely, Sophia. We sometimes think that polluted water is a modern phenomenon, and if we lived more naturally we would not have to go through all this purification and care around water. We see ourselves drinking pure water from pure streams in some sort of pre-industrial Eden. Well, as far as I can tell, water has always been something that requires thought and consciousness. It can rarely be taken for granted – there is either too much or not enough, or the water that is there is not drinkable, for one reason or another. The element which is most associated with unconsciousness is something that we humans have always, in the past, had to be very conscious about.

Even in our own times, we are probably pretty unconscious about water – it just arrives through the tap ready to drink and with no apparent work to get it! Certain communities within society have, over the past ten years, become conscious of the impurities in the water that comes through the taps, and are resorting more and more to bottled water. I can see many of you are carrying your own private supply, as am I! However, our easy access to water that is, in general, very safe for us is still assumed as our right. We don't know that this is a privileged experience, not shared by most people on the planet now or in the past. So we drink it, wash ourselves and our objects in it, swim in it, and in general take it for granted. It is interesting that with water shortages we can no longer be as unconscious about it. And that is as it should be. If we are seeking individuation, enlightenment, wisdom, compassion, awareness, whatever you want to call it, we must become conscious and appreciative, wary and respectful of life and everything that grows in water.

Mythological water

Water has long been used as a symbol for the generation of life, and has been usually associated with the feminine. If we think symbols are generated from physical reality, then the association of water and birth is the foundation of this. But our physical reality may not be our only source of symbol-making. Whatever the case, female goddesses seem be associated with water in most traditions. Astarte's original name was "Womb" or "That which issues from the womb". She was thought to be a goddess of fertility, and was associated with everything to do with the generation of life. Ishtar was called the "All-Dewy One". Aphrodite was born from the sea. The Babylonian mother goddess Tiamat – her earlier name was Nammu – was the primordial water, the "Great Deep". Danoura, a very early Sumerian goddess, was mated with Ea, who was worshipped in the Babylonian city of Eridu and was considered the source of the "Water of Life". Danoura was mated to Ea in his aspect as Lord of Wisdom. Wisdom and water are often connected, aren't they? There is some kind of wisdom in water. The idea of achieving wisdom and oneness move together.

Erich Newmann says, in his wonderful book, *The Great Mother,* "The Great Goddess is the flowing unity of subterranean and celestial primordial water, the sea of heaven on which sail the barks of the gods of light, the circular life-generating ocean above and below the earth. To her belong all waters, streams, fountains, ponds, and springs, as well as the rain. She is the ocean of life with its life- and death-bringing seasons, and life is her child, a fish eternally swimming inside her, like the stars in the celestial ocean of the Mexican Mayauel and like men in the fishpool of Mother Church – a late manifestation of the same archetype."

Aren't these wonderful images? And they are contained in the waters of our collective memories. Each of us "remembers" – through the waters of our bodies – the long story of the creation of life of which our life is a drop, containing the whole. The myths that come down to us have been the ways we told these story to ourselves.

Audience: You can't forget the Virgin Mary!

Darby: You are right – I can't! She too has many names, and one of her most powerful is Stella Maris, star of the sea.

Philosophical water

Thales, whom many consider the Father of Greek Philosophy, and others consider the Father of Science, lived in Miletus, on the coast of Asia Minor, in the 6th century BCE. He lived in personal and collective circumstances in which he had much time for reflection. He is credited with developing the notion that there was an underlying order, both rational and self-generating which informed the multiplicity of life observed and experienced by us. There was a fundamental something, an *arche* – see our word archetype there? – which composed and informed all things. He is quoted as saying, "All is water, and the world is full of gods." Others came after him and gave primacy to one or another of each of the elements, and eventually in the 5th century BCE Empedocles put forth that the four elements, fire, earth, air and water, were the basic components of all existence. Love and Strife, he said, bound and separated them. He is thought to have originated the notion that our bodies are composed of these elements in different proportions and our perceptions and powers are conditioned by the balance of these elements within us.

Interestingly enough, Jung referred to the archetypes as the "forms or river-beds along which the current of psychic life has always flowed." And of course we get our notion of the collective unconscious from him – expressed through the idea that we all share a common memory that is most often shown through our dreams. Our personal and collective memories interweave in various ways and I think we can feel their interweaving in the actions and reflections of our watery selves.

Audience: Doesn't the idea that people dominated by one element will have very different perceptions to those dominated by another, come from Empedocles?

Darby: Perhaps, but it is probably more accurate to say that he is the one who comes down to us as originating this notion.

Audience: Jung's four functions must stem from him too. There is so much work done on the intuitive, sensation, thinking and feeling types and how one type will find another difficult to understand.

Alchemical and religious water

Darby: Jung writes about water from alchemical imagery. He refers to the *aqua permanens* as something akin to "spirit in matter" – the essence which hides in matter. Even from a physical point of view this is interesting, as we are said to be 78% water. Water is the hidden element in our matter.

Christianity uses water imagery in many ways. Christ is the "Fisher of Men". Christian baptism is baptism by water. "Verily I say unto thee, except a man be born of water and of the Spirit, he cannot enter into the kingdom of God." We could spend a long time reflecting on this. Jung said, "Water is the living grace of the holy spirit," and, "Flowing water is the Holy Spirit."

Water has always been used in initiations. My direct experience of this was in Africa in work with the tribal priests and healers. There too, water was the final and greatest initiation. The great witch doctors, those who became legends, had often walked into the river or walked into the sea and returned years later in some other form. So a water death for a witch doctor was not considered the same thing as another kind of death. It showed he was taken directly by and to the ancestors. A water death proved he had served the ancestors and his community well.

Audience: Do you know that the Aztecs were able to "chant" the stars by seeing them reflected in the lake?

Darby: What a lovely ritual.

Psychological water

Psychologically we can think of water as representing the desire to return to the womb, that place of nearly undifferentiated security and safety – for some of us, at any rate. As Howard [Sasportas] used to say, "Not all wombs are five-star wombs." Presumably five-star wombs are those in which the containing water is a place of complete safety and comfort. But even if it is not emotionally a comfortable place, remember all those tiny little hairs we had all over us when we were a foetus in the womb, and how their constant movement and constant moving contact with the womb fluid gave us a sense of total oneness with mother.

For both Freud and Jung, who were great delvers into mythology, the symbol of water was inevitably associated with mother. In *Symbols of Transformation*, Jung writes: "In the Vedas, the waters are called matritamah, 'most maternal'. All living things rise, like the sun, from water, and sink into it again at evening." He also tells us that large expanses of water, lakes or seas, signify the unconscious in dreams and fantasies. And he reminds us of water's association with death. "Born of springs, rivers, lakes, and seas, man at death comes to the waters of the Styx, and there embarks on the 'night sea journey'." He says, "Those black waters of death are the water of life, for death with its cold embrace is the maternal womb, just as the sea devours the sun but brings it forth again."

Audience: Is that where you took your title from?

Darby: You mean, from Jung? "The Womb, Death and the Dream?" Well, maybe partly, but more likely from T. S. Eliot's *Four Quartets* – specifically "The Dry Salvages". I came across it last week and saw where the title for this seminar might have risen from – though it wasn't conscious. In any case, that section of the *Four Quartets* is all about water – do read it when you get home. I'm sorry I didn't think to bring it today. Jung also uses these words constantly in relation to water. I think it is that the symbolic fields of Cancer, Scorpio and Pisces simply evoke these words.

Audience: Water must be associated with feeling in Jung's four functions, although water people are always said to be intuitive.

Audience: Intuition is fire, though, isn't it?

Darby: Yes, water is associated with feeling. Yet I do find it difficult to fit the four functions neatly into a chart, according to the elements. Don't you think it would be a good topic for a thesis? Are any of you thinking of that? I'd love to see a really good study of that. You might come up with some surprises.

Audience: And there are the four temperaments: sanguine, melancholic, phlegmatic and choleric...

Audience: Water is phlegmatic, though if you saw my Cancerian husband running his business, you wouldn't think so. But there is this underlying feeling that draws downwards, no matter how much activity he generates. An inwardness.

Darby: Yes, gravity seems to play a large part here. The melancholic earth type and the phlegmatic water type seem most effected by gravity.

And finally, as we said earlier, water is associated with reflection. And reflection is associated with the life of the soul. Remember Hillman's work on the Neoplatonists, and his development of the notion that it is soul's power of reflection that turns events into experience? We worked with this idea in the seminar on the Moon and on the progressed Moon.

The etymology of water

Let's look at some of the words that are associated with water's action, such as the word "dissolve". In Michel Odent's book, which I mentioned earlier, he writes about water healers. His way of describing them made me think that he was describing a "solvent" sort of person. So I looked up words such as "solve", "absolve", "dissolve" and "resolve". They are all watery words which come from *solvo,* in Latin, which is "loosen, undo, free, release, exempt, dissolve, break up, separate, relax, weaken, cancel, remove, destroy, solve, explain."

Most of the words can be associated with astrological water. One of these led me to "involve" and "evolve", and when I looked up *volvo* I found it was associated with the Sancrit *varas* which meant "circumference" and the Greek *eluw,* "to wrap", and was defined as "to roll, turn about, turn round, tumble" and "to turn over or revolve [in the mind], to ponder, mediate or reflect upon, to consider." This contained both the notion of the circle – water's attribute of self-containment and always turning inward if it can, and the notion of reflection, which is associated with memory and soul life.

Audience: What about the similarity between the Greek and Latin words for mother and for sea? Not in English, but in French,

Spanish and Italian, and probably Sanskrit – though I'm not sure about that – the words for mother and for sea are similar.

Darby: Yes, Sanskrit, German, and Anglo-Saxon, too. The root for "sea" has to do with gleaming or glimmering, whereas the root from which mother-words spring is *ma,* which is about making and measuring. Remember the measuring concept to do with lunar words like month and menstruation, when we were looking at the Moon? So, mother, moon, measure. There's no real etymological connection, but it is, as you say, impossible not to notice. *Mère,* mother in French, *mer,* sea in French, *mare,* sea in Italian and in Spanish.

ASTROLOGICAL WATER

Last year, when we were choosing our subjects for these seminars, I decided to do a series on the elements. When it came to choosing the sequence, my first thought was, "Fire, Earth, Air, and Water", following the natural astrological sequence in the zodiac. But then, during a time of contemplation, I came across this diagram from an earlier seminar. It inspired me, as it so often does, to think about the elements from another angle. Let's look at it.

fire	♈	♌	♐
ruler	♂	☉	♃
earth	♉	♍	♑
ruler	♀	☿	♄
air	♊	♎	♒
ruler	☿	♀	♄
water	♋	♏	♓
ruler	☽	♂	♃

This beautiful construction set my imagination going. I am only using the old rulerships here, as I am speaking about something very ancient. As you see, fire and water both share Mars and Jupiter as rulers, but the heart of fire is the Sun and the soul of water is the Moon. This attunes us to fire and water as expressions of the realms that we call spirit and soul. These realms are constellated most directly through our faculties of imagination and reflection. Earth and air are ruled by Mercury, Venus and Saturn, and so can be regarded as that which meets and manifests the imagination, in form and through time.

Water and soul

Now, what can we say about astrological water that we would not say about fire, air or earth?

Audience: Something to do with the Moon as the reflector of the Sun's light.

Darby: Yes, we might say that as the Moon reflects the Sun's light, soul reflects the spirit's light. Soul is the mediator between matter and the spirit, between that which is visible and that which is invisible. So water mediates. It conveys things. Terrestrial water conveys things in literal terms. In the larger sense, oceans and seas and rivers and lakes carry ships and boats and submarines that transport people and things from one place to another. All sorts of other life forms exist and move from one place to another through water. This aspect of itself as a medium of conveyance is shared with the element of air, but we will speak about that another time.

Water has atmosphere. If you know someone and they are watery, you can walk into a room and you can feel their mood if you have feeling sensors. It is not what they say, it is something else, something more subliminal. Remember, water is a medium that conveys all sorts of life forms and all sorts of dead forms as well. Watery atmospheres convey feelings that are based on events long past. An event that is long dead for one person may not be for another.

Water is about soul, but soul is not only about life and health. Where we feel soul in another is not where we necessarily feel health, happiness, integration and success. Where we feel soul is where we often feel what we might call the pathological – the swampy side of things. We don't necessarily want to be around someone when they are in that place, because we may fear the loss of our own souls in that atmosphere. It can seem as if people lose their souls by sinking too much into their own waters. And yet so many people who have suffered and endured through intolerable circumstances seem to be deep with soul. You feel the soul. So the things that happen in your water are the things that seem to animate this thing called soul, which isn't only concerned with a particular notion of life. It is concerned with the mystery of existence, life and death, time and eternity.

Water and emotionality

Audience: Water is the element that describes the fluid part of a person. People with lots of water are said to be more emotional than other people. They respond to things from their feelings. They react emotionally to situations and to people.

Audience: That may be, but they often seem so repressed emotionally, especially compared to fiery people.

Audience: Well it's odd, because I think they often do appear less emotional than other people. I'm a teacher and I notice my "watery" students show their emotions less than those with less water. Those with no water seem to burst out with their emotions in a way the watery ones don't.

Darby: There is something about people with lots of planets in water which makes them appear less emotionally expressive than people with perhaps one or even no planets in water. It can look as though the more water there is, the less emotional the person seems to be. This reflects the notion of water tending to create a circle when it can, containing itself. Yet if you look closely you can see all sorts of things happening. Once you know a water person well, you can see, or feel, all life in there. You can see the constantly changing reflections on the surface that indicate the moving waters below. When you are in the presence of someone whose waters are stagnant, clogged and stuck in a backwater of trapped memory, you can feel their atmosphere in your own waters. You may not be able to understand consciously what the problem is, but your waters are always resonating with other people's waters, beneath the surface of your skin.

Audience: What if you have no water in your chart? I mean no planets in water.

Darby: Your Moon will always register what is happening around you – whether you have planets in water or not. And so a Moon in Aries with no water might respond to hidden but turbulent waters in another with anger, or action. This may seem not to have any direct connection with the emotions of the water person. When you have water planets, they will be directly affected by the water planets in the other person. Your emotional nature will connect with the feelings of the other person. Whether you have enough detachment to read the shifting patterns being constellated between yourself and the other is another thing entirely.

Water is about joy or pain. One is either enclosed happily in an intimate environment with another or others, or one is longing to break out because things have become stagnant. One is safe and at peace, or one is thrown from that peace by events.

One is either immersed or longing to be immersed. Think of the times when you have been so completely immersed in life that there was no separate awareness, and no power to control your reactions. We often seek these experiences – we want to fall in love, give birth, be embedded in a family or community. In fact most of the discontent we experience comes from feeling as if we have not had those experiences or have lost touch with them, or don't know how to have them side by side with our newly found Western freedom. The water experience – if it is truly water – takes away our freedom when we become immersed. It's almost as if when we are in water's embrace we go unconscious, and as adults we both want and fear that.

Water's urge is simply to seek unity. That's all. Its action is to render everything into itself, to dissolve everything. It flows down the pathways of least resistance. It will flow around any object in its path that disturbs its downward flow. It will move around it, go under it, go over it, dissolve it or go through it – just keep going until it arrives at the sea. Planets in water signs are involved in that action. Planets in water houses are having that happen to them. The urge towards union and reunion implies the sense of separation and isolation we experience right from birth. We leave the watery realm and part of us immediately starts seeking reunion again. The longing for that which is expressed by the symbol of water is universal. It takes different shapes and forms, operates on different levels and is constellated in various dimensions, according to its position and condition in the chart, but the longing for that which it represents is common to all of us.

Water and timelessness

Time itself is one of the things dissolved by our water experiences. When we are truly immersed in an emotional experience we lose our sense of time. It can happen anywhere or any time;

in the kitchen, making a cup of tea, making love, or walking in the rain, alone or with someone else. Then there is the moment when you become conscious of this timeless state, when time begins to creep in again, and you sense that its return will end this sense of forever, of eternity. The sense of separation – this return to conscious awareness, which is inevitably painful – cuts you off from eternity and returns you to time. The consciousness of time breaks into the state of oneness and you awaken to your own cut-off and isolated state. For water, it can seem as if consciousness is pain. Do you think this is true?

Audience: The opposite may be true, too. I remember when I left home for university. After the first semester I was walking along the pathway from one building to another when I suddenly noticed that I was free. I was separate. I was no longer sunken in myself and trapped in the painful atmosphere of my home. I had not even known I was so much in pain – but suddenly I was free, and I never went back. I visited them, but I never really went back to that dank, dark atmosphere of stagnant waters. In this case it felt like consciousness and separation were the bliss.

Audience: You are talking about consciousness and bliss, and I think that is the basis of meditation practices. It is by heightening one's state of consciousness that the sense of separation disappears and one feels unity again. That is one of the joys of meditation for me. I have five planets in water, and meditation takes me into that state. Without it my life would be so fragmented. It encircles me with its awareness of the oneness of all life, all existence. My "eye" or my "I" seems to dissolve, and time recedes, too. So I think ordinary consciousness disturbs water, but not this other kind of consciousness that I achieve through stillness. Meditation brings me back into water.

Darby: Well we're here, so here is where we must always begin.

Audience: Our whole way of being is to battle with separation issues.

Darby: That's the thing with water planets. The entire impulse is to create a circle, bring everything and everyone into it. We look at other cultures which seem to include more than exclude, and we feel our separateness more. We see couples or families who seem to be self-enclosed, and we feel alone. We dream of being included, encircled. We dream of unity through our water place-ments. And yet, to become conscious and responsible we have had to leave whatever unity our families offered. We go off seeking another unity. We seek it here and there, become disillusioned, discover guilt, feel isolated and seek unity again. Through disillu-sionment and isolation we develop our boundaries, and then get the edges rubbed off again and eventually are drawn back into the oneness we are seeking in one way or another.

But now I am noticing that those of us who are happier in the air are starting to intellectualise – the lovers of abstraction are starting to hum. I can hear it in the room. Out of our me-andering we seem to have started rising up into the air. Water meandering allows images to rise from or perhaps through the words spoken. For some of us those images may be painful, and so we begin to rise and rise until we are in the air, away from the pain of the images.

Let's plunge back into the water now. Let's look at water's destructive power. It can overwhelm, drown, tear apart with its force, smash, dissolve to nothing. When it has no place to go, it becomes stagnant. Watery planets in action demand intima-cy and contact and closeness. They can also suck the life out of those they seek to draw into their circle, their womb.

Manipulation is a word often associated with water planets – Cancerian parents can weave their children into the fabric of their lives to always keep them close, and Scorpio parents can bind them with power and fear so that freedom seems deadly dangerous. The Pisces web is so confusing that children don't know if they are bound or not. These are the darker pools in water.

Water healers

However, water is not only about destructive manipulation. Water's action can be deeply healing. Cancerian healers can contain you in such a way that whatever technique they are using makes you feel as though you belong and that you have found a haven, so that nature can do its work. Your Scorpio healers are the surgeons – they cut through to the place of weakness and stay with it until it either loses its hold or transforms itself. And your Piscean healers accept you so completely in your weakness that you can let go of the shame of it and dissolve the knots that were held in place by the resistance to having them in the first place. And again, the darker side: you can feel unable to leave your Cancerian healer, scared to leave your Scorpio healer and guilty about leaving your Pisces healer. Getting away from water is no easy matter.

AN INTRODUCTION TO THE WATER HOUSES

In the ongoing story of life, the water houses represent "moments" in which events happen that are connected to the past – one's personal past, one's shared past and one's collective past. These houses tell stories which arise in the present but always return us to another time. These are the haunted houses. I did a seminar here on family karma a couple of years ago, and I called the three water houses the haunted houses. Yes I can see that many of you were there and remember. We developed the theme that the 4th house is where you are haunted by memories of childhood – you can access them by settling into yourself, sinking down and communing with yourself in memory. We looked at the 8th house as a haunting by memories that are also accessible, but you may need another person to help you access them or they may involve the memories of other people. We also looked at it as the "grave space" in which you honour your ancestors. Sometimes you feel bloody and bowed through accessing them, but you also inherit power through them. And the 12th house was the place where the "unremembered dead" had room to roam. And to honour those hauntings, one had to allow fantasy images, dreams and uncalled for drifts of obscure memory – seemingly without roots – to rise to the surface.

You know there is something mysterious and extraordinary about memory. We say we "remember", but what are we remembering? We are also creating when we are remembering. One of the ways of purifying watery places is to give time and space to remembering the past. Planets in the 4th and the 8th and the 12th house require remembering, as otherwise they seem to act in a dismembering way. The cords of memory are plucked continually, and unless we give time to their integration, we are tossed about by them in such a way that we cannot find peace or rest or continuity.

The water houses are where fluidity, sensitivity and containment are assumed (the 4th); personal and private regeneration of unconscious and undigested matter are revealed (the 8th); and weakness, feelings of loss and the real disintegration which happens before a natural death are experienced (the 12th). These are the houses that catch and hold the memories to which we must return again and again. In these houses, we move house, get deeply involved with others and are dismembered and re-membered. We then seek privacy and the space to re-weave our own lives through these experiences.

But often we don't find that sacred space. How many of us have Cancer on the 4th house cusp with a well-aspected Moon as well as Scorpio on the 8th house cusp with a well aspected Mars and Pluto and Pisces on the 12th house cusp with a well placed Jupiter and Neptune?

Some of us live in awkward circumstances, and endure relationships that are full of exposure and betrayal. Sometimes we fall apart, just when we think we need to be most together, just when we feel the need for intimacy and safety – the containment and encircling of ourselves. We are pushed out of our circle by the very nature of the way we behave, by what we might call our "fate". We are haunted by the ghosts of our past who seem to possess us rather than help us. We are kept out of unity by the very nature of the circle that we are born into, by the very nature of our natal charts.

So home may not be a safe place, and the idea of home may not be something you even want. The memories associated with home may turn any house you live in into something far from homelike. Sexual intimacy and the regeneration it can offer may not be possible. And we may not find a safe haven in which to fall apart in our weakness and be taken care of by kind nurses or nuns.

Now, let's look at water through its own signs and houses.

CANCER

This is cardinal water. Cancer is ruled by the Moon. Contained in these waters we are grown from organism to creature. Cancerian energy returns us to the source of our creatureness. We are womb-born creatures, born out of our mothers, out of the sea, out of oneness, out of unity into separation. Cancer represents all that is womb; the womb of our mothers, in which we develop and grow from seed and egg to infant human but also womb as beginning – our origins, so deep in time that they are beyond remembering. It connects us to the place of gestation, to the container in which our life was nourished and protected and held safe until we were strong enough, complete enough, to live our separate and individual existence. Planets in Cancer seek containment and safety and security, but separation is implicit in their action. Everything about the Cancerian archetype has to do with containment and separation. It constellates our earliest memories. When we have planets in Cancer, they describe the threads that are woven into the fabric of our lives which connect us downward, inwards, to the past, to our personal past as well as our collective history. Stories of exile and return dominate our early religious history, our collective mythology. They say something about the nature of being incarnated souls.

Containment and separation are part of the same field in this dualistic universe. Planets in Cancer are always moving towards or away from a sense of fullness or emptiness. Through these planets we are connected to our own deep family roots in very specific ways, and whatever the planet, it will drive us, draw us, seduce us, call us back to our early experiences and push us out from them as well. Planets in this sign work in moonlight, weaving webs that reveal the ways in which we are all the same; where we share the common need to create a space in which we can rest and find safety, nourishment, unconsciousness. This is the space from where we can go out into the dangers of the world to find what we need to keep those in that place alive and safe.

Audience: This sense of the "safe place" that is so strong in the Cancerian theme – does it include people as a "place"?

Darby: Yes, the longing to be absolutely contained by the other and to contain the other is certainly central to this sign. And that reminds me: I want to say something about separation. I have noticed over the years that Cancerians usually have a story about abandonment in their childhood. This is a common feeling with the Sun in Cancer, and you can hear it from those who have other personal planets in Cancer, too. Cancerians are very sensitive to separation, and they tend to arrive into families where they will feel the separation from their mothers very keenly.

Sometimes it is very dramatic – mother goes away, perhaps dies when the child is young. But more often it is less dramatic – another child is born soon after, and the Cancerian child feels the separation from the mother so powerfully that it begins to grow its shell very early. I have a friend who is Cancerian, and a year after she was born her mother had another child, also Cancerian, and then two years later there was a third Cancerian child born, and then three years later the mother died. These three Cancerians are still very close as adults, although they all drive one another crazy and are constantly being hurt by each other. Fortunately, they have all married people who get on with everyone, but the clan is awash with tides of all kinds of feeling.

Audience: Do they have lots of meals together?

Darby: When they are feeling good about each other, they do, but things happen and then they separate for a time, and talk about one another to each other and the rest of the group. Like all Cancerians they feel separation keenly, but when they are happy they merge together, busy as bees, going on picnics and holidays together, all age groups merging – their children, too – constantly eating and drinking a lot, even singing together!

The house, the room, the corner where one seeks containment, safety and security, are Cancerian places. These are the places in which you feel ensouled, not exiled from Anima Mundi, but one with Her. Planets in Cancer always seek to create this place of containment. The intimacy that is created between special friends, the sense that we are enclosed here, safe and secure with each other, belonging to this space that is created between us, is what Cancerians seek. There is a sense of distress when it breaks, when there is separation, because separation is loss of containment. Loss of containment reminds one, in the waters of oneself, of birth itself. Perhaps in a water birth the shock is less profound. But it will come at some point. Fire houses always follow water houses, and the zodiac, remember, is the story of natural processes told in a particular way. So coming out of anything that implies watery containment must always be at least a small shock to the system, even though the shock may be a natural evolution.

In the natural course of events, you are going to be separated from your source of comfort and security. This is a theme recognised by your Cancerian planets, and they are activated by the feeling of separation to seek comfort and security again. Once comfortable and secure, there is something that pushes towards separation again. And so the story goes on.

Audience: I have a very good example. I have a Cancerian daughter, and in order to get her to go out of the house, I have to take the buggy and the whole family – what she identifies as her family, her toys and her dolls – just to go and buy the milk.

Darby: She's about two or three?

Audience: Yes, nearly three.

Audience: I'm Cancerian, and when I was little my mother had a coat and I used to love to get in it with her.

Personal planets in Cancer

Let's think about this particular watery dimension through the action of planets in the sign. When **the Sun is in Cancer**, I immediately look to the Moon. I know it seems a natural thing to look to the ruler of the sign to define the territory more closely, but I have noticed that when the Sun is in other signs I might wander around the chart a bit before looking at the ruler. When it is in Cancer my eye immediately searches out the Moon – it is as if I can't know anything about this person until I find the Moon. Therefore we could say there are twelve types of Cancerian energy. The one thing that joins them all is that their feeling life is very active, underneath the surface, and no matter how rigid some of them may appear to be, holding those feelings in, the daily changing Moon affects them powerfully.

Their atmosphere changes constantly, but it changes in a recognisable way, so that after a time you can feel their weather as they enter the room. Their life is about constancy and change, particularly in the area where their Moon lives. If you love them, then you accept their shifting and repeating weather changes. Their destiny has to do with creating places of safety for themselves and their own, dealing with the feelings of separation and isolation, and returning to or recreating places of safety for themselves. I have a dear Cancerian friend in Switzerland and she has Moon in Pisces. One summer a spider lived in one of the beautiful plants in her house. Each time I phoned her I found myself asking after the spider as well as the cat and family and friends. It didn't seem odd to either of us. I know several Cancerians whose animals are as important as the human members of their family.

Audience: I also know Cancerians like that. But I am interested in what you were saying before about their "weather changes". I think what you were saying is that Cancerians are moody!

Darby: Yes, that is what they say. But I'm trying to avoid value-laden words here – they interrupt the process of feeling one's way into another sign. As the Moon keeps changing its relation to the Sun every minute of every day, so the weather changes in the Cancerian's inner sea. The way they express this has to do with the Moon, its house and aspects. They move from a feeling of safety to a feeling of isolation very quickly – it happens here in present time, but the present moment always sets off a chord that goes all the way down to birth and its separation out of containment. Cancerians have to get used to this happening and so do those who live with them. It can be very rich or very tiring, wonderful or depleting – that depends on other things.

Audience: My husband has **the Moon in Cancer,** and he seems almost completely emotionless. He does get very irritated when things don't go according to his plan, but he doesn't seem to feel a very wide range of feelings.

Darby: What house is his Moon in?

Audience: Yes, well, in the 10th, in fact right on the MC. And Saturn is pretty strong in his chart, too.

Darby: And the Moon in Cancer is very different from the Sun in Cancer. Moon in Cancer has a life which is concerned with nourishing others in one way or another – it does seem to be a very self-contained Moon, mysterious to itself and others much of the time. But one might say that about all three of the water Moons. Moon in Cancer circles around its hearth and becomes prickly if it feels invaded in any way. It is very busy taking care of everything and doesn't like being disturbed. It develops self-defensive habits very early, so that it can keep circling around its hearth self. People who come into its emotional field are there to be fed, but it can feel cold if there isn't some fire around to heat it up. In the course of my exploration I noticed that Tchaikovsky, Fauré, Satie, Rossini and Debussy all had Moon in Cancer.

Audience: Beethoven, on the other hand, had no water planets at all!

Audience: You once said that **Mercury in Cancer** has a photographic memory.

Darby: The memory and the senses seem to be closely interwoven. Information gets drawn into a web of connections that resonate on different levels of memory, and somehow this makes the past easier to access. It might be that information rides on subtle emotional currents, and when the information is needed later, the feelings bring it up. If Mercury is the information-gathering service of the Sun, then this Mercury brings a very detailed web of information with each new move the King makes! We will see this Mercury in action when we look at a particular chart later today.

Audience: I have **Venus in Cancer**. My other personal planets are airy, and I still surprise myself with my own need to feel that the people I love belong to me. It is square to Neptune in Libra, which is trine my Moon, and so I really think of myself as free and unpossessive. Then suddenly I notice these feeling which arise and are so strong, and I become so protective of my child that it shocks me. Or I can suddenly feel so lost, and imagine I am alone, when in fact it is only that my husband is not emotionally connected to me at that moment. It keeps surprising me, but then my Moon is in Gemini, so I guess everything surprises me one way or another.

Audience: I have Venus in Cancer, but I have a Leo Sun, and sometimes it feels like this really wimpish part of me that I try to hide. My feelings get hurt really easily, and I notice I sort of whinge around my girlfriend, and go all hopeless and helpless. I hate it!

Darby: I would imagine having Venus in Cancer is more awkward for a Leo than for a Gemini, and generally more awkward still for a man than a woman. We are still contained within our society's *mores,* and although there are some biologically based archetypal and universal images of male and female behaviour, a lot of our notions come out of our societies and the times in which we live.

Audience: Jung was a Leo with Venus and Mercury in Cancer. He didn't seem to have that negative side of Cancer.

Darby: I wouldn't be so sure at all. The house or houses where Cancer lives in our charts, and the planets we have there, are very private. His Venus-Mercury conjunction was in the 6th, which is a fairly private house. From what I've heard, he felt very neglected at times in his life. He could be wonderfully supportive and nurturing to himself and others, but he could also be very despondent and moany.

I have used this word "neglect" here, which I normally associate with the hidden side of Pisces. But I have noticed that although Leos with Venus and/or Mercury in Cancer have a particular gift for paying attention to the needs of others, they can also neglect those who feel dependent on them. And I imagine that you have the tender sides of Venus in Cancer too. Shadow and light show up very clearly in people who have Leo and Cancer together in their charts.

Audience: I am a great cook, if I say so myself, and my girlfriend forgives me everything when she comes home after a long shoot – she's a photographer – and I have done the full romantic meal bit. To be honest, I tend to do this only when I feel I might be slipping out of the centre of her attention.

Darby: That is charmingly honest! If we think of Venus as the way we attract and seduce others, then this makes sense. Why would you have to seduce someone who is already there? Venus talks about the dance of love. In Cancer it reels in the net, and then loosens it, so that it can feel the separation and union. Depending on other things, this works well or not in one's life.

Audience: Mars in Cancer is a whole different territory, isn't it? I am an Aries with Mars in Cancer, and I find that I feel irritated a lot! It is such a natural response to anything opposing me, or I should say anyone, like my husband or my boss, or even my son, whom I adore. It's as if I am always fighting shadows. I am wondering now if the shadows I fight come from my past. I never seemed to be able to get a grip on who my father was. In a way, he wasn't there, certainly not so that I could feel his presence. He was someone I had to move around to get where I wanted to go – now that I think of it, sidling around his presence like a crab – escaping him, which is something I got very good at.

Darby: That is very interesting. Most of the people I know well with Mars in Cancer have Saturn in Cancer too, so I am not sure I really have a proper sense of Mars alone in Cancer.

Audience: I have Mars in Cancer in the 12th, which represents all kinds of things I most dislike about myself. When I get angry I cry. When I get hurt I either run away or I pick at the other person until they scream. Actually I can do both together. I send endless faxes to my friends but won't answer the phone until I have got my feelings back in order.

Darby: You're in pretty good company – Picasso had Mars in Cancer in the 12th. He had rather a stormy family life behind the scenes of his Leo rising. Mars is in fall in Cancer, and those who have it can feel it. However, I have rarely met people as actively kind – you with Mars in Cancer, no matter how aspected, do really go out of your way to care for those who touch your maternal heart. You are intensely active in support. This is Mars in a cardinal sign. But it is also distinctly "touchy". It seems driven to connect with that which makes it feel secure and familiar, and yet, once it is relatively safe, it drives its security away. Or it runs away itself, if only for a time. Mars reacts to the feeling nature described by the natal Moon, its position and aspects. Think of Picasso again, with his Moon in Sagittarius in the 5th house – his coming and going, warmth and hurt, and his "touchiness" with his lovers and his children.

We've touched on each of the personal planets. Now, let's look at **Saturn in Cancer**. It describes a two-and-a-half-year period in society when security is threatened in such a way that it is felt directly within family systems. And so those who are born into this time have a sense that their container must be absolutely secure. But it never feels quite secure, of course, because our Saturn territory is where we are off balance and have to work to get to a position where we begin to take responsibility for finding some sort of balance. Emotional and material security are serious issues for people with Saturn in Cancer. They can feel contained within whatever makes them feel secure, but also trapped within it. The work on one's character and life requires facing this paradox. There is a feeling of such vulnerability when their security is threatened. When that shell is stripped off, Saturn in Cancer feels naked indeed. So the need for security is a life project, and the desire to separate from that need, either unconsciously or consciously, is the other side of it. Saturn is in detriment in Cancer. In an ideal world there should be no barrier to intimacy, no striving for perfection in the home, no judgement when it comes to feelings or mothering or how we build our nest. A sense of inadequacy around these things creates all sorts of problems. For Saturn in Cancer, these problems demand work.

Audience: What about Jupiter in Cancer? You can't leave that out!

Darby: Well, I could, because it is so hard to say just a little about it. I think one could write a whole book about **Jupiter in Cancer** – as one could about Saturn in Libra. The signs of exaltation are so interesting. Jupiter in Cancer is a feast. It is like having a room in your house where there is always the possibility of a feast, because in that area of yourself you are always ready to create the feast. Of course it can be overwhelming. Those with it can provide such a rich container on so many levels that it is hard to leave it, but it is a problem of abundance rather than a problem of lack. Whenever you have planets in Cancer, to understand them at all, look to the Moon, always, no matter what the planet. And with Jupiter in Cancer, the Moon will tell you what is being protected underneath the largesse of this planet. Jupiter in Cancer's wisdom is that it knows that by caring for others in a certain way, life will take care of you. But it can also lose itself in its ability to care for others, by becoming a sort of icon of feeling. People with Jupiter in Cancer lose their feeling of security when they don't feel the rhythm of emotional tides between themselves and those closest to them. Being cut off from emotional contact can, for a time, cut them off from the feeling of being spiritually nourished.

Cancer rising

When I think of Cancer rising I think of big kitchens. While the party goes on in other rooms, the Cancer rising people carry on their conversations in the kitchen. If the rising sign is one's natural approach to life in general, then this sensitive and often prickly Ascendant seems to prefer to approach things from the physical source of nourishment in their homes – from the kitchen!

Of course, with anything Cancerian you look at the Moon, and the Moon will tell you what sort of things touch off the sensitivity. It is really a cliché to say that home is very important to Cancer rising, but it is true. What is also true is that home is where the Moon is. And it is the position and condition of the Moon that determines the nature of the sensitivity and the way they express it. Cancer Suns know they are sensitive. Cancer rising doesn't always know how easily touched or hurt or moved they are. Other people experience the effects of our rising signs – in this case, the sudden withdrawal or defense.

The 4th house

The 4th house, Cancer's house, describes our early life, the home in which we were nurtured until we were ready to leave, or not, as the case may be. The sign on the cusp tells us something about that early environment. The planets ruling that sign – in whatever house or aspects they may be found – tell us how and where that early background influences us for the rest of our lives. When we are working with our own personal past, seeking the roots of our present behaviour, we look to the 4th house. The images and memories that arise as we track backwards through time will often circle around planets in the 4th house, or the rulers of the 4th house. These planets carry the secrets of our deepest notion of "home". And home is something that we are always trying to leave or come back to. So planets in this house speak very powerfully in the chart, and the rulers of this house tell us about our beginnings and endings in a very specific sense.

Audience: For example?

Darby: Give *me* an example.

Audience: Well, I have Saturn in Aquarius in the 4th.

Darby: All right, this might say that your first memories have to do with awareness of responsibility. With Saturn in the 4th we usually identify with the burden that was being carried by our father in our early years. In our work with ourselves we have to sort out where our own responsibility lies. It lies with our family, of course. But unless we develop consciousness of where our boundaries lie with our family of origin, we end up with a generalised weight of responsibility to everything. We are haunted by responsibility. Are you part of the Uranus conjunct Pluto in Virgo group?

Audience: Yes, and it is in the 11th house opposite Chiron in the 5th in Pisces.

Darby: So your notion of responsibility extends to wider networks than your family of origin, and can sometimes become a feeling of responsibility for the world – for saving it.

Audience: It is a big theme in my life.

Audience: When it becomes overwhelming you might need to develop the habit of returning to the memories of childhood and the frailty of the child you were. I am looking at Chiron in Pisces in the 5th house. You might mentally work your way to setting up clear boundaries around your present task and how it might help balance this sense of burden. With Saturn we have to be prepared to work consistently at things; we have to develop the habit of work. Saturn in air has to do it in some sort of logical fashion.

Audience: I have Jupiter in Aquarius in the 4th – as a contrast – and I have spent my life running away from my family and trying to recreate a new family, through friends. I am very happy about my background in general, though it was pretty traumatic in places. I think it gave me huge creative scope – though I never quite live up to my own expectations in the end, and I can't stop imagining that one day I will. I really love having friends to stay. But I love it just as much when they leave and I am free again.

Audience: With my Saturn there, I get really edgy when friends come to stay. I find I have all kinds of rules that I didn't know I had. That must be the tyrannical side of Aquarius.

Audience: With my Jupiter in Aquarius there, I never have anyone to stay that isn't as wacky as I am! Oh, and that idea of endings and beginnings – I think I am always off on the next project within a few days of ending the old ones. I love coming back home to rest, but I find myself thinking about the next plan quite soon after landing.

Audience: I am sometimes afraid that I will end up alone, because I read that Saturn in the 4th ends up alone. Is there any truth in that?

Darby: I have a friend who is seventy-seven, and he has Saturn in Libra in the 4th. He is sometimes afraid of being alone in his old age, too. I have pointed out to him that some people might consider that he is already in his old age, but he's an Aries and he looks shocked when I say that. He is very gregarious, but in the last ten years he has chosen to spend more time in his country house, away from the city, with his young wife. I have another friend who is nearly seventy, and she chose to leave her family and friends and go off to live alone years ago. But people do go to stay – though she lives in a house which is too small for guests, so they have to stay in the village nearby. Some people with Saturn in the 4th seek some measure of aloneness in old age; some do end up "alone" and don't like it. Let us assume, because it is more useful and practical and we don't know in the end, that one has a choice as to how this aloneness is cultivated. Learning to appreciate aloneness is good practice anyway.

Audience: What about the father and the 4th house?

Darby: The 4th house is often associated with one's father. With Sun and/or Mercury there, it is important to know something about your father's beginnings to understand yourself. His past effects your notion of yourself. You don't have to know the details – unless you are a Virgo, I guess! – but at some point in your life it is usually important to find his past in yourself. It will fill out your sense of identity. But with any planets in the 4th – check out your father's story in light of whichever planet you are looking at – you will often find clues to your own sense of what is home and what you are creating or seeking, through connecting with his life.

Planets transiting the 4th house

When we have planets transiting the 4th house, we know that certain patterns will be constellated in our present that come from our earliest environment. The past and the present weave themselves together. The result of this weaving can sometimes change the way we remember our childhood. And that effects the way we move forward from the present.

Remember, what happens here touches what we call the roots of our being. Planets transiting the 4th house are like visitors who come to stay for a time. The character of the visitor and the length of his or her stay can change the way we experience life from that time forward. Every year when the Sun goes through your 4th house, some of the atmosphere from your early childhood will rise up into the present. Every year, if you pay attention, you can lay a ghost or two. Every twelve years Jupiter returns to your 4th house. During that year, whatever else is happening, you can bring forth some treasure from your childhood experiences. Every two years when Mars goes through, you can sweep like a warrior through your present home and clear stuff out. We'll talk about the outer planets later in the day.

SCORPIO

Scorpio, ruled by Mars and by remote Pluto, is a water world, but this is water under pressure. It is water at extremes, boiling water, or at the opposite end of the scale, ice. In this hemisphere it is the energy of late autumn. So the wind and the cold blow off and freeze everything whose dying time has come. The leaves are blown off the trees, revealing the clear lines of the branches against the sky. By killing outworn life, the way is cleared for the new life that must have space in which to grow. In the Southern hemisphere everything is starting to blossom in Scorpio time. The death-time of nature is deep within, hidden from view. But it is there.

In terms of birth, you might say that it is associated with the moment when the cord is cut. The relative safety of the womb is truly a past event. You are on your own and now must fight for survival in any way you can. The sense of being cut off from complete nurture constellates a feeling of abandonment which sits at the bottom of experience and becomes a source of much turbulence in the life. That turbulence can, and often does, fertilize deep transformations that change the values and orientation of life completely.

Planets in Scorpio are like laser beams that hunt and find the weakest points in any system, the piece that must be cut away so that the whole organism can live. The ways in which those with Scorpio planets use this energy depends on other things. Isobel Hickey, one of my teachers in America in the 1960's, used to say that it all depended on the "stage of evolution you have reached" as to how you would use Scorpio's energy. It certainly depends on something deep in the soul of the person with these planets. It can make for great power in the best sense. This is the energy of the detective, the psychoanalyst, the psychologist, the surgeon. These planets require people who are able to find the weak points and reveal them, offer space for transformation, or cut them out.

There is a feeling of power connected with Scorpio planets. What is this power we sense, this undercurrent? Let's look at this moment of cutting the cord. Here you are at the border, on the edge – you are connected to a life support system, and then cut off from it. You have to start breathing on your own. Scorpio is about that moment between life and death – where life is cut off, but instantly grabs hold in a new fashion and with new and unknown possibilities. This life out of death and death out of life is so natural and so mysterious.

Sex is as natural and mysterious. Two people come together, are united in body and spirit, whether they know it or not, and out of this comes the possibility of new life, absolutely new and totally unpredictable. Both people are forever changed by the new life that is born. This is obvious when it produces a child – but it is potent on another level even when it does not.

Every act of complete surrender to another produces something brand new, unknown, infinite potential. This is the true alchemy that all alchemy is seeking: to create something extraordinary out of the most ordinary materials. Two people – most ordinary – can, in spite of themselves, create something absolutely extraordinary. The search for this possibility is the secret of Scorpio's power, for good and for evil.

Scorpio water is compelled to penetrate the most hidden places in its search for the point of transformation, where new life can grow from the death of the old. In doing so, it can destroy all sorts of things along the way. We are not always conscious or clear about what we are seeking – these planets are driven by a deep memory of being cut off, but also set free. These pools, where death and life are bound up with each other, are in the depths of each of us, far from the light. People with planets in Scorpio have an unerring instinct about what it is in the other person that is hidden and therefore vulnerable when exposed.

Scorpio is notorious as a dangerous sign. Tell someone you are a Scorpio and there is a *frisson* of one kind or another. But it also has an incredible capacity for intimacy. All the water signs tell us about emotional intimacy. They point to the secret places in ourselves which are revealed to others in certain and very specific circumstances, and the secret places in others which are revealed to us. Intimacy, a water word, can only be felt when a secret is shared. This instinct to feel into the secret recesses of another, where hidden memories lie, hidden traits that have been buried, hidden wells of energy that are tangled up with complexes that mask deeper resources – these things are recognised at some animal level between people. Scorpio's nature is to penetrate into these places, and equally to be penetrated as deeply, and herein lies the source of its reputation. But herein lies the source of its incredible capacity for intimacy, too.

Audience: What do you mean by that?

Darby: Remember water's natural tendency to create a circle, to turn in towards itself. Think of those with whom you feel intimacy. Sometimes you can feel intimate almost immediately with someone you have just met – you are enclosed in a circle together in a crowded room. This is because something has fused, merged between you – you feel touched in a way that goes beyond the superficial circumstances. But it is not always pleasant, this sudden feeling of intimacy. You can meet someone and feel them reach beyond your conscious will into the places where your private self resides. You may not want them there, but they have felt below your surface, and made you aware of a part of yourself that was hidden until a moment ago. And what is this hidden something below the surface that Scorpio touches?

Audience: Something to do with sex and death, no doubt.

Darby: Probably, often enough. Scorpio children connect to the hidden stories going on behind closed doors in their early life. They stumble across feelings and events that are behind closed doors, and this emotional knowledge is both exciting and frightening. But it threatens the child's feeling of centrality, and that produces a strong emotional reaction - the sense of being cut off again. Sometimes they carry secrets that often stay buried until they are activated by other people later on. This activation produces an intense reaction, of one kind or another. This feeling of being cut off can also be activated by the child "stumbling upon" the intimacy that is between its parent, or parents, and another child in the family. This can feel like abandonment and can rise up again in other relationships. Jealousy is part of the Scorpionic story. Someone else has what I need to survive, so I must do something! In an otherwise gentle nature, this urge has to be suppressed, sublimated, transformed. I have seen the most astounding generousity in people with Scorpio planets - truly unpossessive and free of jealousy - but this was won through experiences that generated the most powerful will to overcome these traits. When the will is activated to the good, there is no more powerful will.

And when someone with Scorpio energy goes for holiness, they go all the way, too. When they go for personal transformation, they go all the way for that. It is as if the shock of the loss of connection - Mars and Pluto rulers - is so great it galvanises a huge amount of energy. That energy drives towards some kind of death where one will not be cut off any longer. Remember that this is water and it has water nature's inclination to go downhill, overcoming every obstacle in time, until it eventually finds the sea and is united with its greater self. The soul that is being forged in Scorpio rises out of the encounter with those obstacles. Obstacles are its crucible, its alchemical retort.

Audience: I am interested in this idea about the fear of the cord being cut. My daughter has the Moon in Scorpio, and whenever I was intensely engaged with someone close to me, like my mother or my boyfriend, she used to just burble and chatter, to get in the way of that. Now, as she is older and more articulate, she will actually say, "Stop talking to Richard, talk to me." There is no ignoring that. Even if you say, "Not now," your attention has been drawn to her just by the way in which she has spoken.

Darby: Children with personal planets in Scorpio are very direct in expressing their need to be closest to the source. If their mothers are their source of sustenance, then nothing must get between them.

Audience: My Scorpio son is obsessed with magic at the moment. I am sure magic has a natural attraction for Scorpios. He also has Mercury in Scorpio, but 25° from the Sun.

Darby: I agree with you. I think magic has a great attraction because they know that the real nature of things always contains mysterious processes. There is such an awareness of the mysterious ties that bind, and the innate struggle for existence, and so the magical realms have a great attraction. There is also a feeling for the magical power in relationships. Planets in Scorpio are moved to find the key.

Personal planets in Scorpio

When **the Sun is in Scorpio**, then the person is born during the time of year when, in this hemisphere, the cold is traditionally coming on. It is a dense time of year, full of intense activity. People rarely go away on holiday, during late October into November. There is a feeling of concentration – preparing for the long winter. And people born into this time are born into this intensity and take their cue from it, so to speak. The Sun in Scorpio indicates a destiny where intensity of focus is required. That which demands deep concentration and focus is attractive to this Sun. It shines more clearly in difficult circumstances than in easy ones. It is drawn to people and places where the challenges offer a chance for transformation.

The dramatic stories of murder and mayhem, dying for love, killing for love, Romeo and Juliet, are the stories we don't necessarily want to live, but they are the stories of what happens when the need for this particular kind of intensity is not made conscious. And we, with our consciousness, read these stories with fascination and, albeit vicariously, experience some of the intensity through them.

Mercury in Scorpio feels a lot of the threads that go into making one incident. It senses the complexity of life and will hunt ways of articulating this complexity. But nothing will be easy to say – people with Mercury in Scorpio seem to find rather obscure ways to say things that might seem simple to others. But they often have a natural gift for explaining very complex concepts and situations in a clear and simple way.

Audience: My eight-year-old son is a Libran with Mercury in Scorpio, and he wants to be a detective when he grows up so he can fight injustice. He is also becoming an amateur magician!

Darby: That makes sense, doesn't it? They are natural detectives – always on the hunt for the hidden bit. He must love finding out how to do the tricks and then figuring out how to fascinate others with them. **Venus in Scorpio** is hunting, and waiting at the same time, to find a love that will consume the person completely. Love and magic are wed here, and when the magic is good, it heals the deepest wounds and transforms both people. No half-measures – be loved by this person and you will know it. It is Venus dipped in the waters of the Styx.

Marry someone, or go into a financial partnership with a person with whom there is an emotional connection and, at some point of crisis, those qualities which are hidden in the shadows, will be revealed. The hidden qualities may be wonderful or terrible. What is revealed, however, changes both of you. People don't usually lend money to strangers without heavy contracts. People who have been friends for years often fear sexual intimacy with each other because they are aware that it will change everything. Friends are also often wary of going into financial partnership, when they have had a good relationship that has lasted for years. Any planet in Scorpio may be drawn to these experiences, but Venus in Scorpio wants and needs such experiences for the forging of its soul.

Mars in Scorpio is interesting. When you see it in a chart you know that this person gets really angry only occasionally, but anyone who experiences it remembers it. I have seen it in very passive or sweet natures, and when it rises up it takes your breath away, not because it is noisy, but because of the bone-chilling feeling of it. The capacity for emotional endurance is legendary, but when they decide to let go, they let go fast. There is a mysterious power in the memories that drive this Mars, and depending on the ultimate aim of the soul who incarnates with this formidable weapon, it is a powerful force for good or for ill.

I always think of **Jupiter in Scorpio** as very sexy people. And yet I have known at least one celibate with this position. If Jupiter is well placed, it gives an extraordinary depth of understanding and passion for nature, human nature included. It's as if people born during the years when Jupiter is in Scorpio are given a glimpse into those things hidden beneath the surface, and an ease with things other people find mysterious. There usually seems to be an underlying ease with situations that other people find terrifying – a sort of *sang froid* with murky depths.

Audience: That's a great description of my partner with Jupiter in Scorpio in the 8th – he has a sort of *sang froid* with murky debts.

Darby: Neat twist there – but it's not what I said.

Audience: I know, but it was irresistible.

Audience: Speaking of debts, what about **Saturn in Scorpio**? I have it, and someone once told me it was a heavy karmic debt, or something like that, and it makes me very uncomfortable.

Darby: Saturn is the place where we have to keep working and paying attention to ourselves in all sorts of ways. One of the ways is in relation to others. Saturn, the great teacher, is somewhat heavy-handed in the realm of Mars and, we assume, deeply resistant to the more remote but powerful rulership of Pluto. This placement is hard to penetrate, as well it should be. When you see it in a chart, move carefully, as you are dealing with someone whose underwater caverns have been carved out by profound and often harsh experiences.

They will not show their depths easily – they may not want you anywhere near their vulnerabilities, and they may demand that you stay firmly on your side of the boundary. True contact means commitment to these people, and may feel very risky indeed. Through experience they learn not to play lightly with that which belongs to Scorpio's domain. They take sex and money, magic and power seriously. Those with Saturn in Scorpio who dare to plunge into the maelstrom of intense emotional commitment go through character transformations that turn them inside out and render them incredibly useful to life. If they ever feel betrayed, it cuts deep. There are times when they have to work long and hard to transform a negative feeling memory, so that the waters of their emotional life can flow again. Those who are able to contain and also release their deepest feelings develop the ability to channel their huge resources of energy into building lives through which others are profoundly nourished.

We will look at the outer planets in Scorpio later. It is interesting that we are experiencing all of them through Scorpio during the later half of this 20th century, isn't it?

Scorpio rising

This is a very powerful time of the day or night during which to be born. Deep transformational forces are at work and when you enter through this gate you come in with a powerful drive to live. Your life is a series of transformations. Once you achieve something, it becomes a field from which you will go on to achieve more. The sort of achievement that fires you up depends on other things, of course. Mars inspires you to take action according to its position and aspects at certain times in your life, and Pluto says what will be transformed in the process.

Audience: That could sound like the Sun in Scorpio. What is the difference between that and Scorpio rising?

Darby: Scorpio Sun will work through the house it inhabits, and so the power of endurance, the ability to transform situations and the intensity of response expresses itself through that house. The fear of being cut off from nourishment, and the drive to work with essentials and eliminate all superfluous or outworn material from their lives, centre on the affairs of the house.

With Scorpio rising, it is the instinctive response to life, and one's personality, that go through periodic transformations. The possibility of being rejected, betrayed or abandoned is encoded within the field of the personality. They learn fast to build defenses and marshal weapons that can protect themselves. People with this rising sign experience what it is to feel destroyed and reborn. They rise out of the ashes of these experiences with so much strength that they seem to gain an almost magical power, often over others, and less often, but more significantly, over themselves. These people do grow and change, and it is their personalities that become vehicles for powerful transformations in others.

The 8th house

A person with planets in Scorpio will be attracted to people and events that set off their own deep waters. When planets are in Scorpio's house, but not in Scorpio, events will be constellated and things will be uncovered which may be foreign to the person's nature. Depending on the planets involved, the person will have to deepen their perceptions or understanding, skills or defenses, and perhaps their wisdom to deal with the experiences they encounter. Once the person begins to explore the patterns within their own life they begin to gain the depth to negotiate within very complex situations. An extreme example would be John Kennedy, with all his Gemini planets in the 8th, "playing" with the Mafia before he was elected president. We can assume that he didn't really know the power and ruthlessness of the people he brought into his life, or perhaps he thought he had enough tricks up his sleeve to keep himself invulnerable.

When people with planets in the 8th house come to me, I enter that territory with great care. I don't advise entering that house with heavy boots, as the secrets contained in those planets are deep and complex, and oftentimes the person himself or herself is not conscious of what is contained in the field represented by those planets. They have felt and seen things in their early years which resonate each time they're involved in a close personal relationship, or in any partnerships where important things are shared. Be aware that when you penetrate beneath the surface of this person, you may set something off that you might not be able to control. And if you have 8th house planets yourself, then in working with other people your natural inclination will be to penetrate beneath their defenses and find their weak spots without perhaps meaning to. You have to know yourself pretty well to take that on. Otherwise, in seeing the secret motives in others you will also unconsciously expose your own secret motives to them, and accusations will flow back and forth between you like rapids.

Planets in the 8th house get into repetitive patterns – the same situations happen over and over. I have a secret feeling that this has to do with its connection to "the dead" – there are ghosts to be laid and rituals to be performed so that you don't get caught up with "dead" patterns from your own past or that of your partner. If you have 8th house planets, I think it is up to you to deal with any repetitive patterns that arise in your partnership life. With all the water houses, one is connected to the soul of others. With planets here you might have to pay attention to your partner's psychic "inheritance" as well as your own. I think it must have been easier when people went to church together every week – somehow the attending of that sort of ritual must have helped release difficulties. One always prays for one's dead in church rituals. How do you remember to pray for your dead without that weekly reminder? Our culture has lost touch with its old binding rituals and has not settled, consciously, on new ones that keep people aware of the flow of time through the generations. We'll find new ones. But in the meantime our ghosts are floating around a bit.

Audience: I have noticed that, with planets in the 8th, you keep repeating the same thing over and over, and then, somehow, through the repetition, a breakthrough occurs.

Darby: 8th house people have profound breakthroughs, like water breaking through rock to form a spring on its way to the sea. A client with Venus in the 8th went through years of jealousy; she struggled with it so much until one day she told me, it simply died. "I looked at my son and his wife and it was as if a light went on – I was no longer jealous of her and I could suddenly see she really loved him. I was free."

The cusp of the 8th house, and planets in it, will say something about the atmosphere around sexuality and the atmosphere around money in your home and in your early conditioning. As you know, these placements also talk about inheritance.

8th house matters have been having a hard time staying behind closed doors recently. I imagine it's all the Aquarian energy about. We are endlessly looking beneath the surface of things, trying to pry secrets from Nature, Man, Woman, Matter, Spirit. Everyone is busy trying to see what is really going on behind the appearances. It is fascinating, but what do we do with these secrets we find? So often we start messing around, manipulating, trying to control and direct operations because what we discover doesn't seem good enough. People with planets in the 8th can become so obsessed with seeing through people and events that they can destroy the mystery and vitality of the relationship between themselves and the person or event. And yet, having planets in the 8th means that one must penetrate beneath the surface of appearances – that's what the 8th house is about. Perhaps the secret of this water house is the development of courage to face whatever symbolic realm is represented by the planets in that house. But also, one does usually have to consciously abandon the desire for that which is constellated by the 8th house planets at some point in one's life. Planets in water houses will always tell what has to be washed away. 8th house experiences come through intense personal relationships.

The 8th house is about the nitty-gritty of partnership, as much as anything else. It is where we "share goods". The sign on the cusp and planets there will say something about how we do that. Entering the secret realms of another person and exposing your own secret realms is always a transformative experience; with 8th house planets some of one's greatest acts of courage are the most private. If you want love to stay creative between yourself and another person, you must move with respect into the hidden secret realms of the other person. When the wind blows in November it only blows off the leaves – it doesn't blow the whole tree down. Well, not every year!

Audience: I think, with planets in the 8th house, you are sort of practicing Scorpio – like living in a country with heavy weather when you might come from a country with very light weather, if your planets are lighter than Scorpio.

Darby: Nice! We could use that analogy all the way through here. It is interesting, isn't it, the difference between the planets themselves in a sign and the house that represents that sign's experience? I think of the quadrant first when I think of a house. The 8th house is the deepest part of the realm of personal relationships. The 7th house is where the relationship gets underway, contracts are made up and ideals are stated, but the 8th house is where our blood is the ink that signs the contract, and the ideals are pushed to the wall. We show ourselves to each other when there is attraction enough, and our projections mesh with one another. We really get into the depths of each other with our 8th house planets. Or not, as the case may be. And then we search for a wider perspective in the 9th house.

I spoke of John Kennedy's chart a few minutes ago, with all his 8th house planets. I don't have his chart with me, but he had five planets there; three in Taurus and the Sun and Venus in Gemini. He didn't have any planets in Scorpio. He was brought up in an environment where there were huge issues of power, secrets behind closed doors, and complex relationships that went back generations. His ancestors were part of the interwoven threads of his life. Complex strategies had been developed to keep the lines of power alive through each successive generation. All these "complexes" were his inheritance – let's say they were the atmosphere into which he awoke, being such an 8th house person. His brother Robert was a Scorpio, with an 8th house Mercury in Sagittarius – and so he tuned into similar complexes within the family. I can't remember Teddy's chart – only that he is a Pisces.

Audience: He has Moon conjunct Neptune in the 8th house, opposite his Pisces Sun.

Darby: Well, there you are. People with planets in the 8th house will be brought into experiences where sex and death and power games have to do with money and survival, and they have a deadly serious undertow. What I am saying here is that those with 8th house planets are brought into awareness of these realms very early, and they "notice" these dimensions in significant relationships through their lives. They will be attracted to persons in whom they feel these dimensions operating – so they will be aware of power plays that others make, sexual energy that others exhibit, money games and the most complex and hidden dimensions of ancestral urgings. They will get experienced in recognising these dimensions, but how they navigate them depends on many other things. They will not so much live out of these realms – as planets in Scorpio will – but they will "activate" them in others and learn to navigate them through experience. They will be drawn to those places in people where the complex hidden life and death urges meet and manifest in their multifarious ways. And they will deal with those things according to their own natures.

Planets transiting the 8th house

When planets go through the 8th house, one can feel taken over by something – a kind of haunting that must be dealt with in one way or another. Or a relationship may constellate earlier unresolved relationships. One becomes obsessed for a time. If one navigates the obsession, keeping an eye on the waves from the pilot's box, then the experience can be interesting as well as all-consuming. If you have airy planets or a Uranian distance on things, that is possible. But even with that, the experience of the 8th house is, for those who do not live there natally, all-consuming.

When the quicker planets move through, then you are brought into some sort of local crisis, and the solving of it releases you for some wider experience. When Jupiter moves through, it is a year of the possibility of release from entanglements, financial and sexual – past hauntings. When Saturn spends its time there – a two-and-a-half-year stay – it grinds into the various crevices of your intimate relationship life and demands a conscious reckoning, a balancing of accounts. You are forced to pay attention to those secrets you may normally ignore, and to pull very private dealings into shape.

Now we have arrived at Pisces and it is time for lunch. And doesn't that say something about Pisces? It comes at the end of most astrological discussions, and it comes at the end of the session, the end of the morning, the end of the day. One's consciousness is already moving into another realm. It is the ultimate mutable sign. We will shift into another gear now, and return to the waters of Pisces at two o'clock.

PISCES

As I was saying, Pisces is the ultimate mutable sign. It contains all of that which has come into being and is now being dissolved, so that the traces can be drawn and reshaped into something that becomes new life, new creation. And yet, for this to happen there have to be mists and clouds – it must happen in a realm where the rest of us, the rest of ourselves, cannot go in and busily interfere. This is a part of the story of life that takes place behind doors – like anything in the watery realms – but here, even the doors are unseen. In the Cancerian realm you can see the door – it has a sign saying Mine or Ours. With Scorpio you may not see the door at first, but when it slams in front of you or behind you, you are ready for change. The Piscean door keeps moving its location and it keeps changing shape and often surprises the Piscean as much as the one who has been shut in, or shut out.

Because of these things, I don't think that Pisces is as much about abandonment and separation as about neglect. Planets in Pisces indicate early neglect, and not necessarily because the parents were unkind or cruel in any conscious way at all. It is often that the child with these planets simply seemed to disappear at times; it is their way of responding to certain kinds of difficult emotional situations. Pisces learns very young that the world is mysterious, and the best way to survive is to be invisible at times. Those who cannot do that, because of other contradictory themes in their charts, become incredibly helpful to those who seem weak or helpless in any way.

Pisces planets carry the memory of something beyond memory, something hovering beyond the borders of consciousness, and this memory of other realms hurts, but there is often a secret and familiar joy there too. When they fall into experiences where they can lose all self-consciousness, they are in bliss. They know that this is the only place to be. This seems to speak of the Neptunian side of Pisces.

Many find the pathway to this place in service to others. Some find it in meditation of various kinds. Others find it in drugs, alcohol, and other substances that blur the boundaries between ego-self and otherness. Physical illness or ego weakness sometimes draws those with strong Piscean traits into experiences that give birth to compassion. And compassion is the most deeply nourishing and useful outcome of water's longing for unity. True compassion may be the rarest human achievement, and yet it is something we all experience at moments in our lives, no matter how hardened we may have become to the suffering of others. Here is another of the paradoxes contained in the watery field of Pisces. Something that is so universal in human experience is also one of the rarest treasures of the soul.

Remember that Jupiter is the ancient ruler of Pisces, and it brings its sense of humour to this secret and subtle sign. Moving around the people and places where neglect has been a theme, there is a side to Pisces which finds the way things work out both hilarious and sad. The Piscean sense of humour is born out of an often too intimate knowledge of helplessness and confusion – either its own, or other people's.

Audience: I have a friend with four planets in Pisces, and he is a wonderful companion – when he is around. But he periodically just disappears. All of his friends find this distressing, and he won't really explain it, but he eventually appears again and we carry on being friends. But it makes me wary of him too.

Darby: I spoke of the feeling of neglect that Pisces can experience, but it is true that others can also feel confused and neglected by people with a strong Piscean emphasis. There is this tendency to slip away that runs through everything Piscean. Like all water, it first slips into all the cracks in the armour of those it is attracted to. Then, when it has soaked up some of the pain of the other person, it starts to feel distress itself. And so it quietly begins to withdraw, and this is hardly noticed for some time. Then suddenly, one day, your Piscean companion slips away. You have no idea why. Your Pisces friend was feeling neglected. Sometimes it is simply that they have been neglecting themselves, and so they disappear to return to find their own soul again. Sometimes it is because they have felt neglected by you, and though they never told you, they somehow felt you should have known. They want to be fused with those they love, and also, they want to be free to change shape when they need to.

This sense of paradox runs through everything Piscean. It is the last sign of the zodiac, and so everything is worn away here. All divisions and distinctions are to be blurred until there is nothing left. The commonalitiy of all things – not just all people, but everything – is recognised and accepted in this sign's domain.

When people with Piscean emphasis are in touch with themselves, they are in touch with the place, or non-place, where everything falls apart and waits for something to pull it into manifestation again. No shape and all shapes live together here, and the forming of things out of seemingly nothing is a mystery that plays itself out on every level of existence. That is why they are both pessimistic and optimistic at the same time. They live in the mutable domain where impossible situations can be resolved perfectly in the twinkling of an eye, and where the most perfect moment can be irrevocably ruined by one false move.

Audience: There is so much paradox there. Pisces knows everything, and yet they seem so naive. There is so much kindness and so much coldness too.

Darby: Pisces is ruled by the very remote Neptune, and so in some ways its concerns are not personal at all. Pisces wants to be contained and merged – it is water – but it also wants to be free. There is Jupiter again. Its desire to be conscious and to be unconscious is constantly shifting back and forth. That's why Pisces is probably the most complicated of the water signs, and the most paradoxical things are said about it – why it can be so cold and withdrawn and unhelpful, and why it can be breathtakingly supportive and forgiving. It is also why it feels as if it knows everything and yet also contains a feeling of deep insecurity. Pisces clients often tell me they suffer from "low self-esteem". I have to say, I am deeply suspicious of this concept of "self-esteem", whether it is high or low. The very nature of Piscean energy is to hover at the threshold between worlds – to contain opposites, to feel everything at once and to honour all the feelings without casting any of them out into the darkness. When Pisces holds itself off from certain areas of feeling, it casts itself out of its own healing world. Its spiritual imperative seems to have to do with experiencing everything so that it can feel with everyone.

It longs for unity at all costs and above all things – this is the longing for the ocean that all water seeks. But notice what happens once the ocean is reached. The water on the surface evaporates and rises into the air, moving with the wind's currents to become rain. That is also something about the nature of Pisces, and planets in the 12th house too. Once in this unity, once dissolved and melted into the environment, something begins to move within it and something new begins to happen. It moves out of unity, unconsciousness and the state of oneness it has sought, and off it goes to find another shape.

This longing for dissolution and unity will express itself according to the planets which are in Pisces. Mars will have a very different way of seeking it to the Moon, for instance.

Audience: Blame the other, blame the world, blame oneself – and then atone and find a way to that eternal space again. I do it through meditation. My Pisces brother loses himself in his painting. We both do it through falling in and out of love. Our parents were Scorpios and we are both Pisces. We are both completely reliable, and we also specialise in disappearing acts, romantically speaking.

Darby: In my notes here I wrote, "Pisces is all longing and resistance." The longing is for freedom from anything which binds, and the resistance is to loss of any kind. There is that in all of us, and where there is Pisces, that is where this most subtle of processes takes place – where, in finally giving up everything, the next stage can begin.

Audience: Cancerians have to belong. Scorpios have to change. And Pisces is about letting go.

Darby: In a nutshell, but let's be wary of nutshells, too. Wherever there is Pisces, there is the call for atonement and forgiveness and the releasing of boundaries and the loosening of ties. This is the last sign of the zodiac. It is the end of the story, when everything is resolved and dissolved and forgotten, and out of which another of the infinity of possible life forms may emerge – first as a tiny spark, a speck in the distance, until it becomes like a comet rushing into manifestation on its way to meet an egg.

Personal planets in Pisces

The Sun in Pisces brings the longing for unity and the sense of paradox right into the heart. The dream of fusion is at the centre of whatever seems to be the goal of life. Between the 21st of February and the 21st of March, the body of mankind gets an infusion of cells whose purpose has to do with diffusing, unwinding, unweaving that which they come into contact with. For a Pisces Sun, the way to the light is through loss. That does not mean that Pisces is more unhappy than other signs – remember it is personally ruled by Jupiter – but it does mean that it must often serve the weakest points in itself and others. Think of our classic Pisces, Einstein, whom I seem to bring into every discussion we have. He had extraordinary constancy in answering the letters of children asking for mathematical help. Think of him spending most of his life searching for something he never found – the unifying principle in matter. And yet, no one could think of him as a despondent character.

Audience: But remember all the years he spent trying to undo the practical results of his mathematical leap of genius – the building of the atomic bomb.

Darby: The heart of the Pisces Sun is the dream of unity, and it will undo whatever it can to find it.

With Pisces, wherever it is, the experience of profound weakness is itself leading to wisdom. You know how these things take time. You have to go a long way into foolishness before you get wisdom. It's where the experience of no-self leads to the ability to be able to identify with any self – with the guy in the cardboard box and the guy in the chateau, and the woman behind the net curtains in the suburbs. All are the same. It is the experience of weakness, of helplessness, which signposts the way towards an awareness of grace in the world that seemingly has nothing to do with your own effort.

Audience: I have **the Moon in Pisces**, and everything gets undone around me. I spend my whole life trying to put things together.

Darby: The Moon in Pisces is completely different. You are also in service to the melting of barriers, but in the emotional realm that has other ways of working itself out. This Moon easily gets into the habit of endlessly serving the needs of others; and depending on aspects, and your own spiritual perspective, that is either satisfying or not. With Moon in Pisces, you are intimately connected to the needs of others, through both personal and collective memories. I'm not sure you can choose whose needs you feel most deeply. Sometimes people closest to the Moon in Pisces feel left out in the cold while a stranger gets fed. This Moon draws you to people far from your own home territory, as often as not.

Audience: Jupiter again!

Darby: Yes, it is always hidden somewhere there when we are in Pisces' domain. I notice it very much with **Mercury in Pisces**. People with this seem to have very logical minds, and yet I can't see the logic behind Mercury in Pisces' logic. Years ago I used to say to clients with this position, "You are fundamentally intuitive." Mostly they would disagree, saying that they were not intuitive at all, but logical. I have watched for a long time now, and I think it is a kind of "natural" logic. They sense or feel the pattern in things – there's Jupiter – and they follow the obvious logical trail.

Audience: Well, what is the nature of logic, then?

Darby: Yes, as I was speaking I started wondering that, too. But if we go off on that train, we'll end up at a station far from our intended goal.

Audience: The meandering nature of water.

Darby: Yes, and this water gets uncomfortable when we stay too close to the known route, doesn't it?

Audience: Watery Pisces meanders in a very different way to the waters of Scorpio.

Audience: Scorpio meandering must be like the meandering of a waterfall, if you can call that meandering. All water is headed for the same place – the sea – but they get to it with different rhythms.

Darby: How does **Venus in Pisces** meander towards unity?

Audience: Speaking as one who has it, I think we meander with endless hope and naivety. I so often don't approve of the people I fall in love with, once I get to know them, but I can't untangle myself for ages. I am always looking for the perfect soul-mate, but I seem to fall for people who are fundamentally weak.

Darby: You must have some Saturn there, to judge the people you fall in love with that way. But I won't ask you about the other considerations in your chart, because you have said something that many people with Venus in Pisces say. So we'll just work with that. Venus in Pisces is often in service to a higher form of love than the one who has it in their chart.

Remember, you are not your planets. Your planets describe so much about you and your life. But often, we don't want to know certain things about ourselves, because they do not accord with our ideas or notions, which are often collective anyway. It's important to understand the outer planets and their collective messages, and how they "infiltrate" our personal boundaries, our personal natures.

Venus in Pisces, being watery, is attuned to the hidden vulnerabilities in others. Whereas Cancer will protect and Scorpio will prick, Pisces will allow. Venus in Pisces is attracted to those who need their knots undoing. They offer complete devotion in such a way that the other's defences can loosen and life can flow more easily. When they are loving, they are at their best, and so they love loving.

Audience: I have noticed that they don't seem to get so fundamentally disillusioned as other people.

Audience: No, we are remarkably good at retaining our illusions against all odds! We might lose them about one person, but we keep them there in the background so we can fall in love again.

Darby: Yes, there is the fascinating dual rulership of Neptune and Jupiter. Neptune seems to inform Pisces planets with mysterious messages of total union, oneness, infinite pleasure if they just follow the siren song. And Jupiter brings a strange sort of confidence, which says, "It will be a wonderful trip!" With Venus in Pisces, disillusionment and disappointment can bring them down temporarily, but never for long. Life is about Love with a capital "L" for Venus in Pisces. Sad or happy, fulfilled or unfulfilled, secure or insecure, love is everything. And though they may not always be lucky in love, they do have the good fortune of not being able to hold on to bitterness or resentment for any length of time, and so they truly do learn wisdom on their love's journey.

I could go on and on about Venus in the sign of its exaltation – its story is so rich and various. But let me move to **Mars in Pisces** so we will not fall into the trap of neglecting any of the positions. It is so easy to do that with Pisces. Whenever I see Mars in Pisces in a chart, a tiny picture of a one-man submarine pops up in my mind's eye. This position seems to describe an underwater warrior prowling beneath the waves, on the alert for invasion of its territory from the hidden depths.

This position is given quite a bad press in old textbooks, but then, so many things are. With Mars in Pisces you have to dream your way to your goal, but unless you can envision your goal as service in some form, it seems very hard to achieve anything that brings satisfaction. One's vitality is mutable, and spiritual vitamins are probably more helpful than physical ones, though nowadays we all need physical ones too.

But with Mars in Pisces you are not necessarily going to achieve anything unless you are willing to meander now and again, and in the end it is often your weaknesses that contribute to your achievements as much as your strengths. It seems a kind of "laid-back" position, especially in a man, but there are depths within depths there, and the most extraordinary richness of resources which really only arise when someone else is in need. And like anything in Pisces, others can't necessarily count on it when they think they should be able to – it responds to subtle cues and does not usually seem self-motivated. The one who has Mars in Pisces is often more surprised about what or who turns it on than even other people are.

Audience: Amen.

Darby: Are you going to say anything more here?

Audience: No.

Darby: Appropriately mysterious. Now, those born when **Jupiter is in Pisces** seem to be born with the proverbial guardian angel in attendance. It softens a hard nature and offers spiritual sustenance to a softer one. It does not seem to bring a specific or material stamp of "good fortune", but it does appear to bring small and great miracles here and there throughout the life. It certainly does not preserve its "native" from unhappiness, but it does give the gift of a sense of meaning, even in times of unhappiness.

It truly does give the grace of kindness – though this may not always be obvious in the personality. However, those with it suffer at others' suffering and the only way to relieve their own suffering is to quietly give to others, so I guess that is why they inevitably seem to get wise in the end in a funny, private sort of way. They are often surprised and surprising, with their generousity and with their twists and turns of fortune.

Now, **Saturn in Pisces** seems to be in a very alien realm. People born during the two and a half years of this part of Saturn's cycle seem to incarnate with some of themselves left behind.

Audience: What do you mean?

Darby: I am thinking of Saturn as the Lord of Incarnation, the Lord of Karma, and Pisces as that transitional moment in the cycle where things are loosened from the web of time. The natural longing for eternity pulls things, events and people into another dimension. I am thinking of Pisces' fragile bridging of time and eternity, and Saturn's insistence on the manifestation of eternal dimensions in time and in matter.

Saturn in Pisces demands that one manifests something that is not calculable. You cannot measure the rewards of Saturn in Pisces' achievement – you cannot really chart the path of it. There is no authority it can bow to except the ultimate and most intangible realities, and so it has a problem with temporal authority, its own or other people's. What are the limits of Saturn in Pisces responsibility? And where can it find its security?

Audience: I am at my Saturn return now, so you can imagine the problems it is throwing up. We are the group with that opposition.

Darby: Yes, *that* opposition – Uranus and Pluto in Virgo opposite Saturn and Chiron in Pisces. Your group is working something out that is more than personal or social – the problems you are struggling with in your own work lives and personal lives are problems that need to be made universally conscious. Robert, you said something so interesting about this the other day on the phone. Can you remember it or say it again somehow?

Audience: Yes, I think so. I feel we long to challenge authority, to fly in the face of what is expected of us. We want to rebel, as your generation did, but we are afraid – we see The Authority out there and we are afraid to stick our heads above the parapet. Perhaps we each have different reasons for being afraid, based in our individual psychological background, but we don't feel confident enough to challenge the things that we know are wrong out there.

Darby: Do the rest of you with this configuration agree with that?

Audience: I do feel like a coward about stating my convictions. I am more able to in a group like this – well, sometimes. But "out there" – and I feel a strong sense of "out there" – I tend to hide out. I am sure about something, but I am not sure what, when it comes to it. I feel very complicated.

Audience: Doesn't the Dalai Lama have Saturn in Pisces?

Darby: Yes, and it is in opposition to his Moon conjunct Neptune in Virgo in the 12th house. Can you imagine how helpless he must have felt when the Chinese invaded his country, the land and its people for whom he must have felt so terribly responsible? And think about the path of humility that he treads, while being such a public figure and carrying so much spirituality. Saturn in Pisces finds its true place via a strange and obscure inner and spiritual road. There is no clear way.

You who came in with that mid-1960's configuration will force awareness of the planetary crisis this configuration points to. You will do it through your own personal grappling with confidence, usefulness, purity, corruption, and the various weaknesses that are inherent in being part spirit, part medium-sized animal. With Saturn in Pisces, one cannot afford to hold onto power, authority or security with too tight a grip.

That which is held too tightly melts like butter in one's hands. I think it may be a question of practising holding onto things with such delicate subtlety that you almost seem to be willing to let them go. So, for example, if you achieve a position of authority, you keep it by always being ready to give it up. It takes a lot of practice to get that wise, but it can make for extraordinary spiritual authority underneath any kind of temporal authority.

Audience: My father had Sun and Pluto in Gemini square Saturn in Pisces. He was terrifying at sussing out when anyone was being sneaky or dishonest with themselves or others in any way. He was enormously talented but a failure in the end, because every time he began to achieve something he decided it was too easy and a trick, and he lost interest in it.

Darby: The Saturn in Pisces bit in that is the awareness of layers under layers, which negate the layers above. In other words, you work to achieve or accomplish something. But once you get near it, you see another level of necessity or another level of what it would mean to achieve that particular thing, and it undoes the determination. That is why one has to find a motive that is deeper than any desire for recognition, that even you can't quite consciously access. You can only feel it and ride it, like surfing in a fog. Good surfers can always get there in the end – they become the wave itself. That's the secret of Saturn in Pisces.

Planets in the 12th house

Audience: What about Saturn in the 12th house?

Darby: Well, what about Saturn in the 12th? Does anyone have it here?

Audience: Yes. Can you tell me anything about it?

Darby: Let's start with the notion that planets in the 12th house are often as mysterious to the one who has them as to others. I think of it as the house of the unremembered dead. The 4th house contains your personal history – through it you can get to the universal. The 8th house contains your remembered dead, and those of your intimate relationships – and again, you can reach through to the soul of the world through these "ghosts". The 12th house is the "quadrant of space" where the ghosts of the unremembered dead drift around. One can get "possessed" by planets in any of the water houses, but it is easier to find who is "possessing" you in the earlier two water houses. The planets here carry myths of much earlier or remote times. Reincarnational images arise out of this house. The actions of these planets are connected with appeasement of acts so remote that you cannot analyse or figure out what it is all about. You can only learn to say some version of "Thy will be done." And to learn to do that properly is a lifetime's spiritual training. But the gift is true compassion, which is a miracle not only for the one who has it, but for anyone who is ever touched by it.

More has been written about Saturn than about any other planet, I would imagine, but this is still and always a mysterious position. How does one work with it? I think you almost have to let it work itself. The whole point of having planets in the 12th is to recognise that you are not in control here. Perhaps when you come up against Saturn obstacles in your daily life – and you can watch what house Saturn is transiting to keep track of the "lessons" you are having and the boundaries that are being adjusted – perhaps the "work" is to learn to recognise anxiety in the face of the day-to-day obstacles and the underlying need to sacrifice and atone for something unremembered. It takes endless patience to work deeply enough to satisfy Saturn's requirements. But then, when the time of peace and at-one-ment comes, the depth of satisfaction is equally great. And then one must work one's way to the next layer. This is sacred and personal archaeology. Every obstacle in life both constellates a vague anxiety and offers a moment of deepening through it. This is a very rigorous position spiritually.

Audience: And Jupiter is the contrary, I presume.

Darby: It seems so – a guardian angel, often enough with bright wings, though it depends on what sign as to how bright or dark the wings. But it brings a generalised feeling of protection and a "rescue at the last minute" feeling about it. Faith is easier here, whereas with Saturn one has to work for it. And yet the tradition says Saturn "joys" in the 12th house, which indicates that its rewards are great – the true capacity for contemplation brings the deepest peace of all. With Jupiter here, one does not work so hard for faith. It is a gift, and one's protector shows itself throughout life in all sorts of strange and subtle ways. I'm not going to go through all the positions here. There are so many good books around. Howard's *The Twelve Houses* is one of the very best.

Pisces rising

Those who are born during the hours of the day when Pisces is rising come in through a gateway of mist and dreams. Often other people see exactly what they want to see in these people, because the mist appears to change shape and colour depending on who approaches it. No matter how forceful the personality behind it, no matter how fierce the intellect, Pisces rising conveys its inhabitant in a modest vehicle. I am not saying that all Pisces rising people are modest – in fact I know one person with it who is inordinately immodest. His Mars in Leo cannot help boasting. However, every time he does it, it is a surprise, because his general demeanor is so quiet. And he is receptive to the subtle feelings in his environment, terribly receptive. It is obvious after a time that his bouts of ego-assertion are necessary for him not to disappear completely in his capacity for invisibility.

Pisces rising can become anyone's myth in a moment, but it changes and changes – a true shape-changer. Pisces rising has a transparency that is intriguing. Of course you must look at Jupiter and Neptune to see the realms this transparency is serving. A Pisces rising person born in a year of a watery Jupiter will serve their environment in a very different way to one born in a year of a fiery or an earthy Jupiter. And behind Jupiter stands Neptune – the background siren call of the generation into which the individual Pisces rising incarnates.

Planets transiting the 12th house

When planets transit through this house, some part of you may seem to disappear for a time. You have to shift your perspective to find out what is happening with that part of yourself. One way to do this is to keep track of the Moon every month as it goes through the 12th, because you may then begin to get a sense of where you are most personally connected to an ancient and secret wisdom, which is normally not accessed or attended.

Personal planets going through the 12th get "undone" or washed out, as they connect with the lost traces of your deepest past. When Jupiter goes through, once every twelve years, you are returned to the place where your guardian spirit dwells, and any prayer or meditation you do during that time redeems lost parts of yourself as well as others who are "lost" in the collective. You may never know what good you do through your prayer or meditation, but the good is received where it is needed. When Saturn goes through, you are brought to the places in yourself where walls have been put up against collective suffering. Your work is to check the openings in those walls, so that you can be receptive to others' loneliness and isolation, and yet not be drowned in it. There are always moments of recognition as planets go through the 12th – touching the secret gift of being incarnated in time, alone, and yet submerged in life along with everyone who has ever lived.

Audience: And the outer planets?

Darby: It would take too long to discuss them in depth here. The one thing I will say is that, when they finally go over the Ascendant and through the 1st house, you only then really see what their effect has been through the 12th house. If you pay attention, you will find that you are are awakened to a whole new world, and these new perceptions of life have opened up undreamed-of possibilities for years to come.

Are you ready for tea? We'll take a break and then look at a watery chart in some depth.

A WATER CHART: MARCEL PROUST

This is the chart of Marcel Proust. Have any of you read the whole of his novel? Have you, Bridget? You seem to be the only one. In French or in English?

Audience: The first in French, and the second two in English.

Darby: Congratulations. How many of you have read at least one volume? Yes, well, that's quite a good proportion of the group. All right, let's look at his chart.

I'll read out the positions so we can get to know it together. He has a full 4th house, as you can see, and all of his 4th house planets are in Cancer! Jupiter is in Cancer, its sign of exaltation, right on the IC. The Sun is conjunct a combust Mercury, and both are conjunct Uranus in Cancer a few degrees on. These planets cover the area between 10° and 26°, and so one or another of them is involved with all the other cardinal planets in the chart.

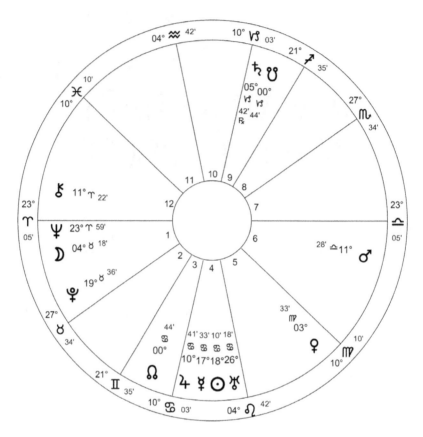

Marcel Proust
10 July 1871, 11.30 pm LMT, Paris
Koch cusps

We see Saturn in its home sign of Capricorn, in the 9th house, conjoining the MC and opposing that exalted Jupiter and squaring Mars, which is quite happy in the 6th but not classically effective in its sign of detriment, Libra. That's interesting, because it is obvious from his life and his work that his illness, asthma, served him well in many ways, not least in giving him the hours of childhood musing and dreaming in bed, and later the excuse to remove himself from society to work. Chiron is in Aries in the 12th house, completing the arms of a grand cardinal cross. But I am very hesitant about using Chiron in a 19th century chart, and so I mention it, but I have not put it in – I don't even know when Chiron came into our solar system! However, there are seven planets in cardinal signs, plus Chiron, and all are linked up in this grand cross. He has Aries rising with Neptune right on the ascendant in Aries, which is square the Mercury-Sun-Uranus conjunction. And, just to complete this orderly and chaotic story, Neptune is also conjunct the Moon in early degrees of Taurus.

Audience: You always use wider orbs than some of us do.

Darby: Yes. In America I was originally taught 10° to 12° for solar and lunar aspects. I have never seen any reason to abandon that habit. I think, when you hear what he has to say about his mother, you might agree that the greater dimension of Neptune in Aries does mingle with his very personal and intimate Moon in Taurus.

Audience: His Moon is part of a very close grand earth trine, with Saturn, Moon and Venus in Capricorn, Taurus and Virgo.

Darby: Yes. All of these planets are tightly integrated, one way or another. Look at that Pluto in Taurus sextile the Mercury-Sun-Uranus conjunction. Other than that sextile, it isn't really intimately involved with the other planets. Well, that's it for major aspects, and I think I'll stick with those for now. We see seven planets in cardinal signs, two in fixed and one in mutable signs. There is one placement in fire (plus the Ascendant), four in earth, one in air, and four in water. This is a very cardinal earth-water man.

He is considered by many to have written the greatest novel of all times. It is three thousand pages long and is called *A la Recherche du Temps Perdu,* translated into English as *Remembrance of Things Past.* Of course, there are those who think it is a huge bore, but no one can deny that it is an extraordinary work. It is a book entirely about time and memory – the greatest epic ever written about the mystery of time and memory. It took the last fifteen years of his life to complete, and he only saw the first part published. As you would expect with his 9th house Saturn, he had to bear considerable rejection before the first part was finally published, at his own cost.

A brief biography

"If a little dreaming is dangerous, the cure for it is not to dream less but to dream more, to dream all the time."

– Marcel Proust

First let me tell you something about the man himself. He was born of a French provincial Catholic father, an eminent physician, and a mother who was the daughter of a wealthy Jewish stockbroker. He went into the military for a year at eighteen and, according to his own account, enjoyed it for its discipline and comradeship. Have you noticed that those who enjoy military life often have hard Mars-Saturn aspects? It must feel secure after the uneven flow of discipline that is associated with their fathers. He then studied law and literature at university – Sagittarius on the cusp of the 9th – and began to write, but events as well as growing ill-health got in the way.

When he was thirty-two, his father died. Two years later his mother died. He was utterly grief-stricken, but he also found himself financially independent. Though he had a very sociable side to his nature and, like most Cancerians, was both very careful financially and hugely extravagant, he became more reclusive as he got older. This was partly due to his asthma, but also to the writing and rewriting, the deepening and texturing and interweaving work of his novel. When he died of pneumonia on 18 November 1922, at the age of fifty-one, he was still writing and revising. The last two books of his great work were published after his death.

Look at that stellium, and the Jupiter opposite Saturn in Capricorn. He was considered by many to be snobbish, undisciplined, lazy and obsessed with both homo- and heterosexuality. His work was considered outrageous in his own time. And yet even in his own time it was recognised as a masterpiece. Somewhere he wrote that "the artist's task is to release from the buried world of our unconscious memory the ever-living reality to which habit makes us blind."

He tells us over and over how memory is evoked, and he also describes how to evoke memory. He uses the smallest, most ordinary objects and events to lead us on a journey through memory and time until – if we are able to stay with him – our very own lives are revisioned and ensouled, as well as an entire era that lived itself out before we were born. He dedicated his life to this, or perhaps we might say his life became dedicated to this. I am not sure how much of his will was involved in it – his Sun is in water, conjunct an outer planet. However, the day-to-day discipline required of him must have involved a great deal of will, helped and hindered by his asthma.

The key image of the whole work comes at the beginning of the book. His protagonist is outside and is cold, so he goes into his house and his mother offers him tea. He doesn't like tea much, but he decides he will have some, on a whim, and he sits down. She goes out and gets a little cake called a madeleine for him to have with his tea. Do you know that a madeleine cake is made in the form of a scalloped sea shell? Could there be anything more perfectly evocative for a Cancerian with a Taurus Moon than a seashell-shaped sweet cake?

He puts a bit of the madeleine onto his spoon and dips it into the tea – it is lime tea, by the way – and when he tastes the cake in the tea, a memory is awakened, and he carries on exploring this for another million and a quarter words. Out of this small incident he weaves an epic which flows on and on through time and memory. In it he includes every emotion, every small object of daily life, every nuance that evokes his time, his era, and the universalities of human life at any time and in any place.

The memory released by the madeleine takes him back to his childhood home and a day during which he had tea with his great-aunt. He remembers that someone was arriving for dinner with his parents. As a terribly sensitive Cancerian child, he found it almost unbearable that he had to go off to bed and be excluded from the dinners and the parties that happened downstairs. All he could think about was the moment when he would say goodnight to his mother and she would kiss him. He found something to focus on, which would return him to his sense of containment, which would encircle him again. It was his mother's kiss. It became, for the moment, the centre of his life – and, through the memories evoked by the madeleine dipped into the lime tea, it showed itself to be the centre of his life in a larger sense.

Audience: His chart is all joined up – like one of those pictures you make from the dots. Everything leads to something else. There is a grand square, and also a grand trine.

Darby: Yes, it is so integrated. Looking at it makes it seem natural that he could weave his whole life into a coherent story.

Audience: Is it about his life? Is it autobiographical?

Darby: No. And yes – only he could have written it.

Audience: Looking at his chart, I wonder if today we would advise him to sort out his feelings about his father, and recognise that he was pathologically attached to his mother. We might have sought to make him aware of his resentment towards his father with that Saturn in Capricorn opposition Jupiter, and both square Mars opposite Chiron.

Darby: Yes and that is one reason why, even today, we must be very careful and very skilled when we use psychological language. From his perspective, he loved both his parents and he never questioned that love. He was considered "odd" – but not because he loved his parents. That is only considered "odd" today! He was strange, according to the social mores of the day, for several reasons that we will not discuss here. He belonged to no circle, yet he moved in many – look at the Sun conjunct Uranus in Cancer pulling him out of one circle and into many. He was an original genius who had an obsession. The writing of the book was his obsession, and in it he wrote about a man who had been a sensitive and obsessive child. The character is fictitious, but it's certainly him. The women in his family were very organised and they had good structures, and he knew exactly where he was. This is described by his earth grand trine of Moon trine Venus trine Saturn in Capricorn conjunct his MC. They were very strict, but he knew where he was with his mother and his grandmother. But his father behaved, according to his memory, in a very arbitrary manner.

Will, fear and longing

Now, the evening in question – the evening his memory takes us back to – tells us all of this. The usual ritual in his home was that he had a fixed bedtime. When it was time for him to go to sleep, he would kiss his mother goodnight, and then he would be able to go to sleep. On this particular night the dinner bell rang and everybody got up from the table, and his father said, "You go to bed now." But he hadn't kissed his mother! And he was bundled off to bed. He went into a kind of shock, because he had been anticipating the kiss so much in the secret part of his soul. When he got upstairs he went berserk – he *had* to kiss his mother goodnight. He *had* to. His circle would not be completed until he had that kiss. His sense of security depended on that kiss. Overwhelming emotion drowned everything except his will – his Mars in Libra – disposited by Venus in Virgo in the 5th, which saw the pleasure of that kiss as the thing that would save him. He worked himself into a frazzle, mentally and physically, by his need of it and his fear of its refusal.

When, later, his parents come up to bed, he confronts his mother, and when he hears his father coming down the hall he thinks, "That's it, I'm finished, I'm dead!" He thinks, "They are going to throw me out of the house and banish me." And, "I'm done for." But he holds his ground and not only wins his kiss, but wins his mother for the whole night. This is because his father, with a god-like and arbitrary decision, responds to his emotion and sends his mother to sleep in his room: "...You can see quite well that the child is unhappy. After all, we aren't jabbers, you will end by making him ill and a lot of good that will do. There are two beds in his room. Tell Françoise to make up one for you, and stay with him for the rest of the night. Anyway, I'm off to bed, I'm not so nervy as you. Goodnight."

Such intense emotion, such will and such fear – can you see how deeply this moment reflects his chart, and how in fighting for his beloved mother's kiss he is telling the whole story of his chart?

Audience: Yes, the ruler is Mars in Libra in the 6th, and he makes himself ill with his longing for specific moments of love – I am looking at that Venus in Virgo in the 5th – and he creates art out of it. And it all centres around his home and early memories which he turns into a wider world, Sun conjunct Uranus.

Darby: But what a battle, with Mars square Saturn and his ruler, Mars, squaring his Cancerian stellium. And we see his burst of courage against what he felt to be terrible odds. And how huge the emotions become with all those Cancerian planets sextile to Pluto, and most of them square to Neptune, fired up in Aries. Venus in Virgo – all that water longing and hunger for containment and nurture through "just one kiss". The sense of being abandoned and the need to fight for inclusion with his Mars in Libra – air – in the 6th house, describing how much his mind was involved in his frailty. And, how much his fear of his father was part of it, with the square to Saturn in Capricorn in the 9th. But oh, how complex we are, and how our charts reveal so many of the layers of our complexity!

He says at one point: "My father used constantly to refuse to let me do things which were quite clearly allowed by the more liberal charters granted me by my mother and grandmother, because he paid no heed to principles and because for him there was no such thing as the rule of law." And that is the Sun-Uranus square Neptune showing. But the Mars in Libra square Saturn shows his fear of his father's law! In his father's mind there may have been "no such thing as the rule of law", but with Saturn in the 9th in Capricorn square his Mars, I would think it was more that his father seemed to act – Mars – in conflict – square – to the "rule of law" – Saturn in the 9th in its own sign.

In his later life he lived in a cork-lined room in Paris, which made his asthma easier. It was because of his asthma that he couldn't even bear to be around the trees which, with his Moon in Taurus, he loved so much. As a true water person with most of his planets below the horizon, he worked all night and slept during the day. His entire household revolved around that. Also, with Sun conjunct Uranus, it makes sense that he turned the world on its head. And, he turned everything into art – Mars, the ruler of his chart, in Libra, the ruler of Libra being Venus, and Venus being in the 5th house in Virgo. Intense sensitivity coupled with a passion for detail was turned into great art – and all in a nest where he could meander down the pathways of memory and re-create his world, circles within circles within circles, including and enclosing and opening out and enclosing again. Water on water on water – Jupiter in Cancer in the 4th at the heart of the stellium with his Sun.

Audience: I have just been tracking his Mars in the 6th house and in detriment in Libra. It is the ruler of his Ascendant, of course. If you follow it around, the ruler of Libra is Venus which is in Virgo in the 5th, ruled by Mercury which is conjunct the Sun and Uranus in the 4th, ruled by the Moon which is in Taurus in the 1st, which takes us back to Taurus-ruled Venus in Virgo in the 5th. Health and work and creativity and home and the past and the minutia of his life and creativity! Once you leave Mars, you get pulled into the Cancer-Moon-Venus dynamic which goes round and round too. So many circles, as you say.

Darby: Yes, that's it. It is very satisfying pulling the threads together like that, especially when you have such a full exposition of someone's life, as we do here, through this masterpiece. I imagine – don't you? – that any great masterpiece contains and expresses almost perfectly the person who has manifested it. It is very satisfying knowing the chart of someone who has written the book or painted the picture or composed the music of the composer you are listening to.

The reclamation of memory

Let me tell you a bit more about what happens next. He goes on for pages about how extraordinary and precious this moment was to him – how he knew it would never, ever happen again. But being a child, and overwrought by now, the first thing he did was burst into tears and sob uncontrollably. He was now further distressed because he felt that this was wasting a huge amount of time, and even worse, it was distressing his mother. He thought she might begin to cry too! That thought was more terrible than anything, because she was a goddess and to see her weaken was almost more than he could bear. It gave him the impetus to pull himself together. You see that Neptune on his Ascendant? I know it is 10° from the Sun and not even in the same sign, but it does sound as though it is speaking again and again. But one way or another, his mother was the centre of his life. His Moon is exalted in Taurus, but that isn't enough to turn her into such an archetypal figure. Perhaps, with Sun conjunct Uranus in Cancer, his Moon was elevated to another realm. We must look at Uranus again, perhaps. Does the very fact of having it in a sign change the nature of the ruler of that sign? I imagine it does, in very personal ways. However, one thing we can connect simply –

his ability to "pull himself together" can be seen in the Moon in Taurus trine his Venus in Virgo.

Let me go back to the original moment here, when he is drinking the tea "in the present" and such rich memories spring up and then disappear. He wants the memory to reappear, and he describes the process of how he gets it back. I want to read it to you, because it is such a detailed account of the reclamation of memory.

> I retraced my thoughts to the moment in which I drank the first spoonful of tea. I retraced. I discovered the same state illuminated by no fresh light. I asked my mind to make one further effort to bring back one more fleeting sensation, and so that nothing may interrupt it in its course, I shut out every obstacle, every extraneous idea. I stop my ears and inhibit all attention against the sound from the next room and then, feeling that my mind is tiring itself without having any success to report, I compel it for a moment to change, to enjoy the distraction which I have just denied it, to think of other things, to rest and refresh itself before making a final effort, and then for the second time I clear an empty space in front of it. I place in position before my mind's eye, the still recent taste of that first mouthful and I feel something start within me. Something that leaves its resting place and attempts to rise. Something that has been embedded like an anchor at great depth. I do not know yet what it is, but I can feel it mounting slowly. I can measure the resistance, I can hear the echo of great spaces traversed.

Audience: I have noticed that the smell of another person, without knowing that we are smelling the other person, can open up a whole host of images that reminds us of someone we knew when we were young.

Audience: I have noticed how this very discussion is meander-ing and yet always returning and encircling the central theme – a bit like the sort of art you are talking about.

Darby: Yes, you are right! But this might be difficult for those of you who are more comfortable with straight lines and who find meandering uncomfortable. Check your water planets or water houses when you are in a situation or discussion which mean-ders rather than goes somewhere straight. Meandering seems to waste time, but it also brings in things that are excluded by going straight towards something.

But to respond to your comment about our sense of smell – and we could include touch and sound, in fact, all our senses – these physical impressions are mixed into the waters of the body very early on. They are then carried in the water and activated by events and people that arrive in our lives at various points. Musing, meditating, allowing or facilitating those states of mind where the past and the present can weave themselves together – this is water work. Those who are debilitated by illness have this process thrust on them. Those who are intensely healthy must make space for this process or else end up losing touch with their souls, and this makes life a very lonely, desolate, and cold place for water.

If we don't know how to take ourselves to a water place, the place where our soul lives, we will be taken there by life. From a Cancerian point of view, we will feel and therefore believe peo-ple are abandoning us – they are not taking care of us. The cusp of the house which Cancer inhabits will tell us where we will feel this most. From a Scorpionic point of view, we will feel and therefore act as if they are out to destroy us. The house where Scorpio lives will be the place where we feel this most severely. From a Piscean point of view, we will imagine that we are not being seen and so feel neglected. And the house which Pisces cusps is where we will feel this neglect and so have to find a spiritual solution. Feelings of loss in these areas of life come up differently in different stages of one's life, and each time they seek resolution through the images of loss which they evoke.

Memory and timelessness

Let me go to the end of the book, where the garden bell that rang in the beginning of the book is re-evoked. At the beginning of the book the garden bell rang, and he is returning to his mother. On the second to the last page he says, "The garden bell in childhood and the bell at the party cast his mind over events from then to now [he is talking about his hero, the narrator]. I was terrified to think that it was indeed the same bell which rang within me and that nothing I could do would alter its gangling notes... [and he blocks his ears to hear it better] in my own depths that I had to redescend and this could only be because the peal had always been there inside me and not the sound only, but also between that distinct moment and the present one unrolled in all its vast length, the whole of that past of which I was not aware that I carried about within me."

The whole world of the work is contained between two images of the ringing of a bell. A bell rings and the book begins. A bell rings and it ends. He tells us of memory which is evoked through our senses. There is something religious about this – but why not? He, with his four planets in Cancer in the 4th and his Moon in Taurus conjunct Neptune in Aries on the Ascendant, brings the most mundane, the most ordinary moments of life into a realm that is bordering on the sacred. He opens up the realm of fire and imagination – through his Neptune on the Ascendant in Aries, so integrated with his personal planets – in a brand new way with his very simple, sense-based, emotionally laden memories.

He speaks of us as being limited in space but being unlimited in time, because through accessing our own memory in the present we are taken into our past. Look at that chart, and look at what he is saying. Through our own past, down and down through time, we contact something vast and infinite. We have everything that everyone has experienced within us, and through going down to our own personal memory, we can then go deeper and be fed by images that rise from even deeper sources. His Sun and Mercury in Cancer are conjunct Uranus. That is where he is speaking from.

Audience: It sounds like he is talking about collective memory.

Darby: Yes – personal memory as access to humanity's memory.

Audience: It reminds me of Jung and his work.

Darby: And he is also not easy to read. Such a volume of work! Think of Jung with his Mercury in Cancer and his Moon in Taurus. Both Jung and Proust open the pathways to memory which open the way to imagination. They do it in different ways. Jung has Sun and Uranus in Leo, square Moon and Neptune and Pluto in Taurus – they are not all in aspect to each other but I am talking about the fire and the water in square signs here. Proust has Sun conjunct Uranus in Cancer square Neptune in Aries which is conjunct Moon in Taurus. Both of these men have Mercury in Cancer and both spend their life looking at memory and the images that rise from memory. They both teach us about how the past weaves itself into our present and gives birth to future potential.

Audience: And in Proust's work it all starts with a sip of tea, the sound of a bell.

Darby: It is all based in the senses. With his Sun square Neptune in Aries conjunct Moon in Taurus, he says our senses falsify the real nature of the world for us. Well, he would say that, wouldn't he? But he has also got hold of something that is universal here. He sees through his Neptune in Aries an archetypal realm which he accesses through his senses with Moon in Taurus. He perceives the difficulty of the fire world – the potential that speaks in images – coming through our senses. He senses the distortion, and with his Cancerian planets he goes through his personal memories to reach that archetypal realm.

He attends his memories, he reflects with his water through his sensual Moon in Taurus trine Venus in Virgo. Water is always reflecting, and it needs quiet time to access what is rising. Water people cannot find peace unless they take time for reflection, time for the images that have crowded the day to rise to the surface and settle again. Remember the little girl with the apple juice? Water needs time to settle after a swirl of activity.

Audience: He has created his own circle through his art – beginning with the bell and ending with the bell.

Audience: I think that this chart is a very beautiful example of Rudhyar's approach to the Moon. Proust's Moon is just past the waning square, heading towards the next new Moon. And his Sun is in the 4th house, which has to do with memory of childhood anyway. I think Rudhyar says that, with the waning square, you find yourself recalling the lessons of your own experience, and that you are trying to find a new essence of meaning. Also, his Moon is just between Neptune and Pluto, and Rudhyar talks about the last planet the Moon contacted before birth and the first it will contact after birth. The previous connection with Neptune suggests a sort of lost memory of something that goes beyond the person and very far back in time. That it is approaching Pluto might describe the obsession to recall it, to bring it up from the depths of forgetfulness.

Darby: That's a fine weaving you have done here.

Audience: These memories that he had about the cup of tea and the bell – was it when he was between five and six years old?

Darby: Yes, Tony, those were the first instances. Why?

Audience: Because I've just calculated that it was the time when his progressed Moon was in Cancer and was approaching a progressed New Moon. So the experience contains the seed of his whole story.

Darby: He is writing this as a middle-aged man who remembers it, and he begins it in 1909. The tea incident occurred early in that year, the characters of his book-to-be arose during May, and he began writing in July. The first draft took three years. He almost married in 1909 – he was very attracted to a young woman – but instead, he retired from the world and began writing.

In July of 1909 his progressed Jupiter was at 18º Cancer, conjunct his Sun. His progressed Moon was at 11º Virgo, entering the 6th house. Neptune, in the sky, was at 16º Cancer. Uranus in Capricorn had just opposed his Mercury-Sun. Perhaps that tells us about his turn of direction from marriage to retreat and this book. While he was writing the book, Neptune was over his Mercury, Sun and Uranus. The first volume was published, at his own expense, in November 1913. He had not fully completed the work, to his own satisfaction, when he died in November 1922.

But let's leave him now and go on to other things. If you ever have a winter free, you might sit in front of the fire and read his extraordinary novel. It is always so interesting to have access to the chart of the one whose writings or paintings or music you love, or even those of whom you don't love. We learn so much from it.

Now, let's think about water signs in non-water houses, and then we will spend the last part of the day looking at the outer planets in water.

WATER CUSPS

Cancer's houses

The house in which the Moon resides shows the area of your life where the memory of safety, security and containment was both established and broken in your early years. It will also be the house that describes where you look to find, or establish, or create this security again. Of course, the sense of security here waxes and wanes. The sign of the Moon says how you respond when the container is felt to be safe, or when it is felt to be broken. And the house where Cancer resides says where you find the home, the container within which and out of which you move to find your daily reflection, nourishment, waxing and waning security and loss of security.

Audience: I can say something about that. I have the Moon in Aquarius in the 6th, and I was brought up by a series of nannies, most of whom I loved. But my security depended on their moods. I have Cancer on my 11th house cusp, and my friends are absolutely my family – I am very protective of them, but then, I have Mercury and Saturn and Venus there too. When I am insecure I become really impossible and though my friends complain of my moodiness, I feel that their love and my devotion to them is my security.

Audience: So, Darby, you are saying that we create a home for ourselves in the house where Cancer resides, and our Moon can then experience its emotions and soul life in the way of the sign and house it inhabits. The house where Cancer resides is where we seek to create a circle, a sphere. You have to leave it, but you always either return to it or make another one.

Audience: I was just thinking that the 4th house must be where the memories of the real early childhood live, and the sign on the cusp takes you to the planets and the house which, as you say, give the details of the story. My 4th house cusp is Virgo, and my Mercury is in Leo in the 2nd, and my father was the headmaster of a good school and so a local figure of respect – and that was a big factor in my childhood. I have Cancer rising with the Sun in Cancer in the 1st, and I am a teacher too, but of children with learning difficulties.

Darby: And your Moon?...

Audience: ...is in Pisces in the 10th.

Darby and Audience: Ahhh.

Darby: Look to the house where Cancer resides, and then to where the Moon is, and you will see where you look for your sense of home. Of course this "home sense" is not always comfortable – and if your early home life was disturbed, as indicated by your 4th house conditions, then the home feeling you create/ discover in each new environment will have some of that quality to it.

Audience: So we will fall into the behavioral patterns of our natal Moon when we are seeking "home" in any new environment – but it is the house where Cancer lives which will indicate how we go about finding this "home" feeling.

Audience: I have Cancer on the 8th house cusp, and Moon in early Taurus in the 6th. One night, about six months after moving into my last flat, I was in the kitchen preparing dinner for a man I had met and imagined might become my lover. He didn't actually become my lover in the end, but I felt the feeling of "home" for the first time that evening. I have Moon opposite Neptune in Libra!

Scorpio's houses

Audience: And what about the other two water houses? Which do you look at for Scorpio, Mars or Pluto, or both? And how do you read that complexity?

Audience: I have Scorpio on the 6th house, and Mars conjunct Sun in Virgo in the 4th. Pluto is there too, but not conjunct the Sun-Mars. I have trouble with my stomach. It flares up when I am working too hard or not working properly. I work at home, of course.

Darby: The house where Scorpio lives is where one has intense feelings that resonate to the "being cut off" feeling, and where profound changes take place at significant moments in one's life, changes that transform one's life. When planets go through that house, both Mars and Pluto resonate, wherever they are. So, for example, a client with Scorpio on the 8th house cusp and Mars in Sagittarius in the 9th travels both for money and for love affairs, mostly falling in love with men who live far away. With Pluto in the 5th in Leo, the underlying hunger is for personal creative transformation in every relationship and every job she takes. She passionately believes in this possibility, not only for herself but for each company she works for and each love affair.

Water feels natural in the 4th, 8th and 12th houses, because these are very private houses and tell us things about the most private, intimate parts of our lives. But as often as not, water signs are on the cusps of the other houses, and so we are vulnerable and private about things that are not naturally assumed to be secret. Cancer on the cusp of the 3rd might be private about relationships with siblings, or with one's reading matter. Scorpio on the cusp of the 11th might be secretive and jealous and wildly protective of one's various worlds, one's networks. Or Pisces on the 9th might be hopelessly romantic about the journeys one never took and the subjects one never studied.

OUTER PLANETS IN THE WATER SIGNS

Uranus in Cancer

Let me say something briefly about Uranus, Neptune and Pluto in Cancer. Many of you have **Uranus in Cancer**. You seem to be experimenting with ways of nurturing yourselves, your families and even your gardens! You cannot rest comfortably in your family of origin – you are early exiles – and as a group you seek to create families out of all sorts of combinations of people. Life is experimenting through you in this way. When the experiment succeeds, it is great – a family that is free and individualistic. When it is going wrong, it is awful – no feeling of family anywhere and "selfish" and disruptive feelings everywhere.

Neptune and Pluto in Cancer

Most of us haven't experienced **Neptune in Cancer** in our life-times, and we won't in the future. It was there between 1901-1914 and anyone with it is in their mid-eighties to nineties. Most people of that generation are gone now, except for some of the very tenacious ones. But some of you have parents or grandparents with it, so let me touch on it briefly. As you can imagine, there is a great wash of feeling for home, country, mother, tribe, because by the time Neptune had left Cancer it was all falling apart and becoming a dream. There was a collective disillusionment and longing for that which once was. Layers of memory sinking and surfacing were part of the generation with Neptune in Cancer. The generation born in the first years of the 20th century saw everything safe disappear in their very early years, and so no wonder they idealised it forever. Pluto established itself in Cancer in the middle of 1914 and didn't leave completely until the middle of 1939. So in the case of that Neptunian generation, the sense of loss was deepened through world events.

Those born during Pluto's transit of Cancer experienced one or two world wars in their own times. **Pluto in Cancer** shows up as wild disruption of the Cancerian symbols of security, complete destruction and transformation of basc linc security. This was a time when we were driven to an awareness of the fragility of things such as family, community, nature and nation – things that were taken for granted in the realms of the unconscious for so long.

Audience: What about Pluto in the 4th house but not necessarily in Cancer?

Darby: We spoke about the void which is in fact at the centre of everything. You know the story – when they broke into the Temple at Jerusalem, and they were finally going to find this god who was so strong and so powerful, and they opened the tabernacle, there was nothing in it. Pluto in the 4th usually indicates something that creates a void in early childhood. It may be something almost historical – events in your father's life before you were born which resonate in your own childhood. In some way you are cut off from your roots through that Pluto, and may feel this void at the centre of things. And yet out of this void, this profound sense of often intangible loss, you may build a life, a world of unimaginable richness. It depends on how you live your life from deep within, whether the centre is empty or filled with the "Divine Nothingness of God".

Pluto in Scorpio

Audience: What about Uranus, Neptune and Pluto in Scorpio? We are living through times in which all of the outer planets have gone through Scorpio.

Darby: So many things have been said about Pluto in Scorpio over the last decade. We can assume some sort of cord has been cut to our racial ancestry, and we are now off on a new adventure. We have had to look at the worst sides of ourselves as a species, and our relationship with the resources of our common "other" – the earth itself. As Pluto has gone through Scorpio and aspected all of our fixed planets, we have experienced various levels of transformation of our resources. Each person who has gone through Pluto transits can look back and see what was taken away and what was uncovered in the process. Those who have followed the trail of the transit have generally seen new life emerging in the void left by Pluto in Scorpio cutting familiar but outworn matter from our lives. Those of us who are still left with a sense of powerlessness in the face of what was revealed through the transit may find that Pluto's transit through Sagittarius begins to drive us toward adventures that uncover deeper understanding of the patterns that inform our lives.

Neptune in Scorpio

The generation with Neptune in Scorpio – many of you here today – carry a collective dream of some sort of renewal that might come from going as deep as you can into that which you feel might drown or transform your natures. Intense encounter offers death of the outworn self, and rebirth of the new bud of selfhood which is more deeply connected to the realities of life. Neptune in Scorpio opens you up to emotions that seem dangerous to ego development, to your sense of identity.

For example, if it is in the 10th house this sense of danger may constellate around one's mother, and then can be projected onto "the world". One looks for ideal situations in which to express one's usefulness to life, one longs for vocation of some sort, but each experience is disappointing in some way. Wherever Neptune is, there is longing and disappointment, if one holds on too much to the concrete things associated with that house. And there is extraordinary grace when one gives up the concrete for the spiritual connection. If you have Neptune in the 2nd and you try to hold onto your property, it slips away. Hold material things lightly and they may come and go, but your wealth will be unending.

Audience: I have Neptune in Scorpio in the 10th house. First of all, I find it easier to cry in a public place than I do at home, and secondly, I find myself saying, as a way of avoiding the fact that this is my personal experience, "I am crying for the sins of the world. I am a channel for the tears of the world."

Darby: But that is also true. On one level it is probably an escape or distortion, but there is a numinous transpersonal note which Neptune constellates that we cannot understand and that gets mixed up with our personal sorrows. We try to figure out why we feel sad and, looking for a reason, we find a personal one. Or, just as you are describing we find a transpersonal one. It's impossible to completely untangle Neptune stories.

Audience: I have a story about Neptune in Scorpio in the 4th house. It was the most fascinating case I have ever seen with this position. It was a chart I did, and he had Neptune trine the Sun in Pisces in the 8th, and the Sun was also opposite Pluto. He didn't know who his father was, but he was quite certain that it was one of three people. He asked me to see if I could tell from his chart. One of them was a street musician, who was also a drunkard.

The second one was a contrabandist who had a boat, and the third one was a policeman. Out of the three I really couldn't tell. It was amazing that the three of them could fit so perfectly.

Darby: Keeping him confused about who his father really was, which was perhaps the point of the aspect in his chart anyway. That's fascinating.

Audience: I am a Cancerian with the Moon in Pisces and Neptune in Sagittarius conjunct the IC. I will always idealise the place where I am at any time as perfect – this is the whole world – especially when I am with my family. But I live in more than one country, and move back and forth. I am very Neptunian. I have not known my father, but I have always idealised him. Also, for me, the past is very mystical. I was never attracted to the subject of history because I could not think of countries having separate histories. I didn't study the history of my country because I thought that history itself was an absurd thing. I thought, "We all come from the same thing, so history is absurd."

Darby: That's interesting as you come from Greece, where some might say that history began! I wonder if what you are saying is part of Neptune's story in Sagittarius?

Neptune in the 8th house has the capacity for touching something that is mystical, that is spiritually "erotic". But the one with it has to be careful not to try to hold onto the elusive quality of what arises there. If you try to keep what you dream of, where Neptune resides, there is nothing but disappointment and a sense of loss. Wherever Neptune is, if you grab for it, it disappears.

Neptune in the 12th house is like having your own private monastery or chapel. You go there to let go of all self-awareness and give yourself over to the dreams that dream through you. As far as I know, the only problem is that you cannot stay there – you have to come out into the hurley-burley of the world.

WATER SINGLETONS

I think we can say, in general, that when you have only one planet in an element, it takes on a greater significance than it might otherwise. When that planet is strong by sign, house and aspect, then of course it increases the weight of it. It increases its dominance. But even when it is not particularly strong by position and condition, if it is the only planet in that element, it seems to live under a pressure of sorts.

Audience: Like being the only water Sun in a big family of fiery, earthy and airy people.

Darby: Very much like that. Any singleton in water must be checked carefully in a chart, as it will be carrying all the water and it is probably "easier" if it has an outlet through earth or even air to allow the emotions to be released through work or art.

Often a person with only one planet in water will appear more emotional than one with lots of planets in water. The very watery people try to find ways to create a circle within themselves, to settle the water. Of course, if you are part of their inner circle you will get swept into their currents and eddies – that is why you were attracted there – but from the outside they often appear cold.

Audience: But I think water is often cold! I think their reputation for warmth is false.

Darby: You may be right that water needs fire to heat it up – otherwise it gets exhausted in taking care of others. And it needs earth so that it can find service that absorbs it and soaks up its emotional energy. And air to ruffle it, to blow it about and distribute it. But we are not all symmetrically fashioned, and people with lots of water sometimes feel as though they are on their own, having to resolve things, to create circles, and to find their own sea with only a little help from the other elements. We are all little laboratories for nature to play and experiment with as she evolves her way towards some mysterious sea.

THE PROGRESSED MOON IN WATER

I am not going to say a lot about the progressed Moon today, as we have spent so much time with it on other days. Just remember that when your Moon progresses into water signs, it is time to deal with the memories that rise through the occurrences of the house it is moving through. The water houses encompass the dimensions of life where feelings and memories are naturally evoked, and where containment and concealment are natural reactions. When you have water signs on these houses, then it is natural to be private and to have emotional reactions to the affairs of these houses. When you have other signs on these houses then you will have other kinds of reactions. When the progressed Moon goes through your water houses, certain memories will be evoked and you will have the urge to react accordingly.

Progressed Moon in the 4th house

Audience: So when your progressed Moon goes through the 4th in Leo, you will feel like re-creating yourself or your home life.

Darby: Yes, and you will look at your home and discover that which lights you up or dampens you down. There will be an urge to create something new out of your history, and in doing so you will find that memories of childhood creativity, or the lack of it, will rise in your inner life. You may want to create a new relationship with your parents or your childhood memories.

Progressed Moon in Scorpio

Audience: My progressed Moon is in Scorpio in the 2nd house.

Darby: When your progressed Moon goes through water signs, there is an internal shift in your perspective. You feel more security- oriented as it moves through Cancer, more intensely focused as it goes through Scorpio, and more disoriented, full of longing for peace, or full of compassion as it goes through Pisces. These reactions are set off by the affairs of the houses where the water signs live. There are ghosts that arise from the houses where water lives. The ghosts live in the things of the house. It may be a time to recognise and lay ghosts that have not been laid to rest. It is a time in which bringing reflection into your daily life allows your soul to inhabit your life more deeply. You will feel strong emotions around the things of that house, because it is full of feeling already, having water signs as rulers or ruling tenants. When the progressed Moon goes through, the feelings wash up from the past to give you the chance to release old memories and lay old ghosts.

Having Scorpio on the 2nd house means that your relationship to the material world is quite intense. Your Mars and Pluto will tell the story more deeply. When your progressed Moon goes through Scorpio and through the 2nd house, then your "close encounters" with others will make you aware of your relationship to your body, your material wealth and your resources. Your feelings will be intense, and early childhood experiences around your possessions will rise up to be reclaimed and recognised. Certain pools of feeling will disappear and you may find yourself thinking, "It always mattered what sort of car I have had, and suddenly I notice it doesn't matter at all any longer." Or the reverse, of course, is also possible. "I haven't cared about pos-sessions since my brother took my teddy bear when I was three, and now I suddenly want my own things!"

Progressed Moon in Pisces and the 12th house

There are layers to the progressed Moon as it passes through the houses. I know someone who is having her progressed Moon through her 12th house, in Pisces! What is she doing? She is visit-ing people in hospitals and prisons every week. These people are releasing ancient traces of sadness and loss in her. She is allow-ing them to pass through her. Her friends can feel a new emo-tional freedom rising in her, slowly, softly, as she goes about her day-to-day life. She is not afraid of giving herself to people who are deeply cut off from society. She is receiving something back that is impossible to calculate. The 12th house is paradoxically the deepest and most shallow to traverse. What you see on the surface is what is happening, but the depths are limitless from our perspective. You can track planets going through it very lit-erally, but also never ever reach, with your mind, the depths of what is really being undone here.

I am thinking of a client who has Cancer on the 12th house. From her I learned that the Moon going through is releasing very personal memories which carry silent, deeper traces of family memory. She is caring for her very old mother now, and she tells me of the memories that "arise from touching her arm as I take her across the lawn to sit under the tree." Whoever you happen to be caring for during that time, your memory images rise and touch the surface here and there as something is being loosened and unbound deep inside.

The house where Scorpio has rulership will be where you react with intense feelings and actions. When your progressed Moon goes through Scorpio, the memories contained in that house are stirred, and waves of feeling arise whenever the affairs of the house are constellated. It is a time when your soul is engaging with the issues of that house in a particularly charged way.

Progressed Moon in Cancer

Audience: My Moon is going into the 2nd, in Cancer, now. My natal Moon is in the 4th. I am becoming possessed by the need to buy objects for my house. It's so obvious that it annoys me.

Darby: Yes, I have been struck, too, by how surprisingly obvious the Moon's progressions are – but of course there are layers beneath, where the interesting action lies. So it goes into Cancer in the 2nd house, and yes, it makes sense that you will be attracted to buying things for your home. Underneath that, there is the recognition of the tendency to seek security through material objects (Cancer on the 2nd). On the one hand, the Moon going through gives you a chance to remember your childhood in terms of the objects that meant security for you, and all the emotional tones that make up such memories. On the other hand, it allows you to feel the emotional depth that matter carries, and how each individual thing has a history and a story. It gives you the ability to recognise what really belongs to you and what doesn't.

With progressed Moon in Cancer in the 2nd, you can navigate your feelings around the need to possess and be possessed by your things and your home. As the memories from the past weave themselves into your present, you can look for the quiet pools in your life where you can take moments of rest. You can find out what really matters, and some of the historical and psychological wherefores and whys. You may find yourself panicky, caught in moments of feeling inadequately resourced, poverty-struck, disconnected from your familiar material world, not feeling at home in your body. When you are able to simply bear those feelings without rushing around, you will find they swirl round a bend and settle. Then you are safe again to feel matter as the sweet earth and as your home.

I'm going to stop now. We are running out of time. Just remember that when you are looking at the progressed Moon in water signs or water houses, you are looking at memories that might want integrating into the fabric of the present. Keep yourself alive to feelings that rise up, and the memories that are hidden in those feelings. Giving them attention weaves deeper colour into your personal tapestry and probably lets old ghosts find rest. These old ghosts are part of your ancestry, and each of us has times in our lives where we must serve the deep past in this way. This is how past and future get woven, through our attention to such things in the present.

I'd like to remind you: when you enter the 4th, 8th or 12th house of another person's chart, go carefully. When you are looking at the houses which are ruled by Cancer, Scorpio and Pisces, allow memory images to rise and attend to them with care. If you are heedless when you enter the Cancerian territory in another person, they will be prickly and retreat into their shell. If you are naive when you enter their Scorpio territory, they will attack you or themselves, and if you are insensitive when you enter their Piscean domain they will disappear and not be available for further discussion.

If you are a watery person and very good at analysis but not very good at allowing fantasy or daydreaming, check out what is happening with those water planets. Somewhere inherent in water is the longing to remember and resolve the past, and dissolve boundaries between itself and others. If feelings aren't flowing, then it's probably worth finding out why. Water teems with life, and so water experiences teem with life too. Water is on its way to the sea, and from the sea it returns to the land, and this long journey is the journey towards self-realisation. This water self-realisation awakens through the multitude of encounters water has on its journey to and from the infinite ocean. The encounters, driven by a longing for union, offer the experiences that will wear away resistance and give birth to compassion. Each emotional experience reshapes the past.

Watery people need time to let the waters settle before moving on to new experiences which offer different shades of emotional intensity. Always, the past is being re-imagined and re-membered by each new experience. If your memories of the past have stayed the same over the years, perhaps your waters have not been moving as freely as they might. If you are repeating the same emotional loops in your relationships, you might want to investigate the watery areas of your chart to see if some of the memories contained in those waters can be filtered through new ways of working, thinking or re-imagining yourself and your life. In the waters of yourself the past is always seeking to flow, to nourish and animate your present and indeed your future.

It's time to close now. Take a moment to gather yourselves together before returning to the other circles you inhabit. Thank you.

BIBLIOGRAPHY

Jung, C. G., *Collected Works, Vol. 5, Symbols of Transformation,* Princeton University Press, Princeton, NJ, 1976

Jung, C. G., *Collected Works, Vol. 11, Psychology and Religion,* Routledge & Kegan Paul, London, 1973

Neumann, Eric, *The Great Mother,* Routledge & Kegan Paul, London, 1955

Odent, Michel, *Water and Sexuality,* Arkana London, 1990

Proust, Marcel, *Remembrance of Things Past: 1,* Penguin Books, 1989

Sasportas, Howard, *The Twelve Houses,* The Aquarian Press, Northamptonshire, 1985

Tarnas, Richard, *The Passion of the Western Mind,* Ballantine Books, New York, 1991

PART TWO

FIRE,
Fire and the Imagination
The Heart of Our Story

This seminar was given on 29 September, 1996 at Regents College, London, as part of the Winter Term of the seminar programme of the Centre for Psychological Astrology.

THE PRIMARY ORGAN
OF PERCEPTION

Today we shall talk about fire. During the day, and through our conversation, we shall evoke this realm, which burns at the heart of all created things. In discussing fire, we shall be talking about imagination, because fire's realm is the imaginal realm. The images that arise through the element of fire speak directly to the imagination and come from the spiritual dimensions where all potentialities and possibilities exist. Imagination is the access we have to the spirit of things. When we were looking at water, we thought about images too, but those were the images which arose from memory, and were turned into food for the soul. Through fire, we are connecting to another thing completely. In the realm of water, the feelings are first, and the images rise from the feelings. Here the images are first, and everything arises from the images. Fire is that which informs us at the very heart of our being. Everything else comes after.

I am looking at fire as the primary organ of perception. The images that arise in the centre of your heart are the images which light up your path. By this light you move towards certain experiences, become who you are, and make meaning of your life.

Let's outline a container for today's work. I want to talk about the history of our relationship to fire for a bit. Then we'll reflect on some of the more ethereal realms of fire, and see how far we can go into the heights that fire can reach. For the rest of the day we shall talk about astrological fire in its different manifestations. I want to look closely at Mars, Sun and Jupiter, and then at the signs through which fire expresses itself most directly – Aries, Leo and Sagittarius. I have two interesting charts to show you, which express the fire theme in different ways. We'll see how far we get with all that, and then what that opens up for us. I was going to say we will think about how to navigate fire, but that might not be an appropriate metaphor here. It may be better to think about how we can navigate the air and earth and water by the light of our fire selves.

There are two things about fire that I wish to have us keep in mind today. The first is that fire, by its nature, consumes and transforms things. The second is that fire is generally destructive if it isn't controlled. These two principles operate on every level, as far as I know – physically, mentally, emotionally and spiritually.

LEVELS OF FIRE

Terrestrial fire

Let's start with material fire, if that isn't a contradiction in terms. In the *Encyclopaedia Britannica* it says the evolution of man could be equated with his ability to handle fire. He couldn't come out of the warm tropical forests until he could keep a fire alive. According to this source, it was around 500,000 years ago that we began to be able to handle fire. The first evidence of this is in China, with Peking man. Other men may have used it before, but Peking man definitely did. Before that, presumably, we met fire as a dangerous and terrifying element. It generates itself naturally through spontaneous combustion, through dry branches rubbing together, and through volcanoes. The sparks generated from rolling stones can get also get a fire going in nature. And then, of course, there is lightning. Do you know that there are approximately 10,000 electrical storms on the earth every day, and there are approximately 100,000 incidences of lightning striking the ground every day? Since it only happens a few times a year in England, it must happen an awful lot in other places. It certainly happens a lot in Africa. When I was there through the 1970's, it was still the highest killer of animals and people in Southern Africa. I wonder if that has changed? Lightning is the greatest natural generator of fire that we have here on earth.

So, we learned to guard and keep a flame from the fires we came across, about half a million years ago, but, we are told, it was not until around 10,000 BCE that we figured out how to generate it ourselves. This period is some time between the Old Stone

Age and the Neolithic Age – the New Stone Age. One of the earliest tools was a pointed stick of hard wood, together with a piece of soft wood with a very small hole in it. When the hard stick is twirled in the soft wood very, very fast, it creates a spark. Have any of you ever seen fire generated in that way? Very impressive. It must touch something very ancient in us – it feels so magical when the spark touches the wool or straw that you have ready.

From about 10,000 to about 7,000 BCE we got some sort of control over fire – we could generate it at will – and therefore we became free to move as far as our legs would take us. We could go into the cold places now, because we could take our warmth with us. Over time we found that we wanted to stay in some of these colder places, and we developed the technology that allowed us to clear land, fashion suitable dwellings and cook food with utensils that we made. Since that time we have been finding more and more ways to use fire power, and we have handled increasingly powerful fires for our own use.

Think of the atomic bomb. That is an extremely dramatic expression of fire power brought into shape and under control by human ingenuity, whether we like it or not. And think of a rocket firing – the fire power that it takes to get the rocket out of our gravity field and into orbit. I am not up on the latest technology, but I am sure fire is being played with all the time, and each time we put our brains to it, we come up with more exotic ways to harness it. Do you know that the simple friction match was developed here in England, in about 1827 – only 170 years ago – by a man named John Walker? We have come a long way since then, and the question is, of course, how well we are able to handle all this fire power.

When it is said, however, that the evolution of man is linked with his ability to handle fire, there is certainly something to it. Let me quote here from *Britannica:* "The modern history of technology and science could be seen as a continual increase in the amount of energy available through fire and brought under human control. Most of the increased available energy has come from even greater amounts and kinds of fire. The control of atomic energy is merely the most recent step in the use of fire for the benefit of mankind." A huge amount of our technology is fire-based, and it is our technology which has brought us to this level of civilisation. I know that we all have attitudes about this level of civilisation, but I am just stating a fact here, not making a moral judgment.

Mythological fire

There have been fire gods as long as we can remember. The Latin *ignis,* from which arrives our "ignite", in turn comes from Agni, a Vedic god who was the messenger of the gods and the bringer of fire. It is interesting that Hermes is everywhere, even in fire. Fire in alchemy becomes spiritual fire, and it is very interwoven into and akin to spiritual water. However, as fire, it requires an "agency of control" if it is to operate fully in accord with its nature. It is said that "common fire" generates nothing but destruction.

In many early religions, fire becomes equated with "the Spirit". It was connected to the notion of the central life-force itself, vitality. The Zoroastrians of Iran worshipped fire as the most subtle and ethereal principle, and held it to be the most powerful and sacred power. They said it was kindled by God and presented directly to man by their deity. Flame was guarded, purified and cared for, long after we knew how to generate and use it. Even as late as the temples of Greece and Rome, it was tended by the Vestal Virgins. When the Greeks migrated from one place to another, they tended and transported the sacred fire of Hestia. Even today, every Roman Catholic church has a perpetual flame. It is only put out when a church is deconsecrated. As long as it burns, the Holy Spirit inhabits the building.

The Siberians honoured their fire god by keeping all filth and impurities away from fires and hearths of any kind. The Aztecs of Mexico and the Incas of Peru worshipped gods of fire with sacred flames that they apparently ignited in a concave metallic mirror by concentrating the sun's ray on it.

It must have been so natural to honour fire as sacred – all those thousands of years where keeping it lit meant the difference between life and freezing or starving to death. All those years during which thousands of generations lived and died and no one could imagine that one day fire would be generated by any man, woman or child. We had to wait for lightning to strike, grab a bit of it, then go off into the wilderness where it might not strike for some time, and where we had to keep it alive or die.

How precious it must have been, how valuable. What sort of man or woman would have been chosen to guard something so precious? And what happened when, through chance or carelessness, it went out? You can see why it still has its magic power for us – think of the incredible feeling a fire in a fireplace gives, or a camp fire.

The dangers of fire

All the way down to our animal roots, to the very beginning, fire has been extremely dangerous for us creatures. I don't know how many of you have ever been close to an uncontrolled fire. I've not been near one in a city, but I have in the bush, in Africa. In the winter, fires rage across the bush. One is constantly putting out fires, your own or someone else's. I remember jumping up in the middle of the night so often, and rushing off to go to help put out a fire on some neighbour's land; getting closer to the fire, the frightening heat of it, and the sense of its potential unpredictability. The danger of it! The excitement of it! And the exhaustion at the end of it, when the fire is eventually under control. Every able member of the community is part of it, every time. Well, those who aren't part of it aren't part of the community. The potential destructive force of the fire binds everyone together – it tests each individual. And at the same time it binds the community, but it is a harsh test, and those who fail in courage are branded by that fire as visibly as those whose recklessness takes them too close to it.

Fire divination

Have you heard of fire divination? There is a divination call *ignis specio* – to see in the fire. Anyone who has sat by a campfire for any length of time can imagine how easily one could develop this with the right rituals, discipline and length of time. Gazing into a fire which has been built and is contained, most of us enter an imaginal realm. Gazing into candlelight settles the mind and imagination too, and brings a sense of comfort that is very different to the comfort felt by water. Both speak to something primitive and deep within us – the realms of spirit and soul.

In a simple way, things get sorted out in front of a fire, if you are able to let it in. A fire can make you cry. A fire can turn tears to laughter. There's something immensely comforting about it when it is contained, and something immensely frightening about it when it isn't contained. Atomic bombs are fire controlled and contained, but they are almost too much fire for humans to deal with and, at this point, they are only used for destruction. Those who support their existence do usually believe their power of destruction is to stop greater destruction, but most of us are suspicious. Nuclear reactors represent fire power too. Again, there is really too much power for us to handle there, at this point in our development. The collective images which arise out of atomic bombs and nuclear reactors are pretty horrific. From these images, we feel that we are playing with more fire than we can handle, and that may be true.

Celestial fire

In esoteric religions, that is, in early Islamic mysticism and early Christian mysticism and in Neoplatonism, fire is the realm which is first in manifestation, out of the unmanifested, undifferentiated realm of being. This fire realm is Plato's realm of Ideas, but these "ideas" are not what we think of as ideas today. Today we would think of ideas as belonging to the air realm. But in early Greek thought, the world of Ideas was the first world available to our perceptions – form, but not yet form. All worlds descended from it. Each created thing has a spark at the centre of itself, that is of the fire. Each manifest thing is a mixture of "creative fire" and the "shape" it takes. This is its "thingness".

The secret of reaching God, or whatever you call the Source of Being, is to find that fire, that spark, in yourself. Once having found it, you must find ways to return to it again and again. In this way you become more "at one" with yourself, more true, more complete. You are the fire in the container, and you are the container. The container is woven out of time and space. Since the astrological chart describes the moment when you step into time and space alone, without guide ropes, we could say it describes the container. The divine spark shows itself through your Sun, it drives you forward through your Mars, and it illuminates possibilities just beyond your reach through your Jupiter.

But you can lose touch with fire, even the fire in your own Sun. Unless you can reach the central fire, the images at the heart of your Sun, then life is a two-dimensional grind. This central fire always illuminates your life. When it goes out, you go out. In truth, it doesn't go out – it goes back, you might say, to its home in the realms beyond form. But that's another thing.

It can seem to go out. You can feel as though it has been crushed by circumstances, by the daily grind of life, by the cruel and harsh necessities of life. But it is always there, burning at the centre. We lose touch with it sometimes. The images reflected in the fire go darker when we cannot find fulfillment through action, when our creative capacity has no outlet, and when we cannot make meaning out of the events of our lives.

This must happen, it seems. It is part of our spiritual life, whether we are conscious of such a thing or not. Bodies get sick and emotions take us through the wringer. Our minds go blank or get filled with nonsense, and we lose our light at times. When we lose that light, it usually indicates that we have arrived at a moment of transition. If we survive the darkness, when the light returns it often shows us a new territory to conquer, a new creative field and another shape through which our hearts find meaning. When St. John of the Cross wrote of the "dark night of the soul" he must have been speaking about this loss of fire contact.

So the fire is always there, whether you have planets in fire or not, whether you are in touch with your "spirit" or not. Images from the archetypal realms are always playing through your spiritual body, and they may be expressed through the mediums of air, water and earth too. The Sun is the source of light for all of us, and each of us carries its light in our hearts. We know our source, we feel the heat from it in our bodies and in our hearts. We know when we are cut off from it – we feel cold in our bodies or cold in our hearts. We know directly, with fire-knowing.

Remember the moment when you suddenly fell in love with astrology? You may have been reading a book about it, or listening to a conversation, or having someone do your chart, and suddenly you "got" it, and you had to get more. The flame leapt up and sent you on a quest, and that quest has now brought in the other elements. You study it, you work with the intellectual concepts that circle the symbols, which you know in your fires – directly – but you have to work to translate them into language, into words that can convey this "fire-knowing" to others. You do your charts, and in the day-to-day experience of this you work the vision into your being and into your life until the vision, the fire-knowing, is expressed through everything you say and do.

The fire has then found material which can express it, keep it alive, and you warm yourself and others in its light.

This fire-knowing has to be translated or made manifest through other elements if it is to be communicated, or be of practical use. But not every fire experience must be brought down into manifestation. There are some instances of this "fire-knowing" – when you are in the heart of a spiritual experience, through meditation, religious ritual, certain types of drug experiences, and those moments which simply come, "when the fire and the rose are one" – in those moments there is nothing to be done. You are so profoundly connected to that which informs all and everything that time and space are no longer your prison.

These are what we call mystical experiences. Everyone experiences this at some point in their lives. What they do with it is another thing. Most people can't leave it alone. They have to turn it into something. St. Paul said that when an insight into the nature of things bursts into your mind, you must speak. Most of us feel the need to translate these moments into words or action. That gives them meaning. It seems as if they demand expression. But I have a secret suspicion that there are certain mystical moments which are best left alone. They come unbidden from the realms of Spirit, and they light up your life forever.

Audience: Are these only available to fiery people?

Darby: Oh, no, these moment of grace can come through water, earth and air, too. The ones that come through fire have a particularly dramatic flavour. That is how you recognise them. You walk into a part of the forest where you see something miraculous, heart-stoppingly beautiful. Or you are waiting for a bus in the middle of the day, and suddenly the world stops and an image breaks through. There is nothing to be done. But if this happens again, and again, then something must be done. It wants communicating. It wants translating.

That is one of the difficulties with fire. You see a vision, you sense the whole in the part, you get inspired and energised. You see the spirit of the thing. Then you try to bring it into your life, express what you saw in one way or another. You tell someone. You paint a picture. You write a song. You start to study astrology. And the work to develop the skills that will express the fire starts getting in the way of the fire. In studying astrology you discover all these contradictory bits of information. And the people who give you the information turn out to be less perfect than you want them to be, and when you try to express your own knowledge it comes out clumsy and you are not understood, or worse, you are criticised. The work of bringing the fire into the world through our dense time- and space-bound selves is not easy.

And yet, this is the work that we call creative – the spark, the vision, and then the years of practise to work it through the other elements so that heat and light animate our existence. Fire is always transformative, but it both destroys and creates. Love often begins in the fire. You meet someone, a spark flies between you, and your mind and body and emotions all start churning around. The fire gets it going. Whether this fire-love turns into something that can nourish your whole life depends on other things.

Fiery people love passionately when the light is bright between themselves and the other. But there are problems in communication that have to be attended to. Have you noticed how difficult communication can be with very fiery people? The fire seems to give such a clear vision of the infinite potential in the relationship that it seems inconceivable to the fiery person that the other is not seeing the same thing. Fiery people imagine that the one they love has the same images in their heart and mind. They imagine that those they love are operating on the same principles.

Audience: And so if I assume that we will both tell each other the truth all the time, and one day I catch him out in a lie, I am not just disappointed in him, I am shocked to my core! I "know" that total honesty is the only way to be with someone I love – no matter how much it may hurt him or me – and so I "know" that he knows the same thing. I am burned by the lies of those I love, if I am fiery.

Darby: Exactly. This is one of the difficulties of fiery perceptions. Similarly, you never know what fiery people are doing with information you give them. When people have strong fiery charts you speak directly to their imagination – they understand everything at once and patterns leap into being through only a few coordinates. You can tell them three facts and they leap to the principle behind the facts. They have highly developed faculties for pattern recognition. Of course what you mean to say is not always what they perceive. And so communication can be confusing. They leap to conclusions and you may find out that what they took from what you said is not what you meant at all!

You tell your four planets in Aries child how rude the man at the supermarket was to you, and the next thing you know, the police are phoning you. They have your kid in the station because he went to the supermarket and starting throwing tins of tomatoes at the guy. Or you tell a client with Sun and Mercury in Leo and four planets in Sagittarius that they "know" the nature of reality directly. You then have to pay attention, because they might have stopped listening while you are telling them how easily this knowing gets distorted and how long practise of discipline and humility are needed if they are not to become destructive and get burned up. The next thing you know, they have started a religion and they are saying to everyone that you told them to.

Audience: You exaggerate!

Darby: Barely. But do you see what I am saying here? Fire responds to the spirit of something or someone. This spirit is translated into images, because the fire realm is the realm of imagination. The whole trick is what you do with the fire, with the imagination. On this earth, fire is not enough, knowing is not enough. We are water and earth and air, too, and in each of us these element are mixed. The fire may be the heart of the mix, but it must interact with the other elements so that food gets cooked, imagined dwellings get built, and poems and songs get spoken and sung.

Let's get down to the simple and obvious notions that centre around astrological fire. We speak of fire as exuberant, enthusiastic, full of faith, confident, zealous, bumptious. What else do we say about fire?

Audience: Fire is positive. Also, thoughtless, heedless and reckless.

Audience: Fire is impulsive, and also intuitive. I was thinking about what you were saying about it coming from images. That is interesting. Do you mean pictures? What do you mean by images?

Imaginal fire

Darby: Okay, back into the imaginal realm...There is a book by Henry Corbin called *Temple and Contemplation.* He is writing about Islamic theosophy, and he says that God, who is the "Hidden Treasure", created creatures to know him. But the intensity of the light (of God) had to be modified if it was to be accessible to perception.

You could say that, to "see" the light, creatures had to be different variations of all light. The *imago* which is projected from this divine and eternal reality would be received according to the nature of the perceiving creature. Nature could be described as different variations of light. The "Hidden Lord" is manifested through the fire in different things, through the elemental fire at the heart of things. Listen to what Corbin says here: "...The light that is the manifestation of this Lord through the fiery nature, through the elemental fire concealed within the signature, is only perceptible to the organ of vision created by that same fire. Like alone knows like..."

This notion is expressed in different ways throughout history and through all cultures that develop their mystical visions into thought forms and rituals by which one can attempt to reach the place of vision again. It can be recognised in the Platonic World of Ideas and the Neoplatonic Intelligible Realm as described by Plotinus. It corresponds with the reality described by saints and visionaries in all ages and through all times.

One function of religious ritual is to create containers in which people can place themselves so as to be receptive to this fire without burning up or going mad. Of course there are other functions of religion that are not so elevated or grand, but one mustn't forget that the high dwells with the low in this world of duality. Religious mystical history is littered with people who tried to "get there" too quickly, or without the proper guidance or preparation. And it is littered with people who received the light and went off on mad destructive missions with it. They were unable to simply be grateful and full of awe.

The highest fire realms demand that you leave your discriminating mind at the threshold. This mind is useful and necessary for part of the journey, but there is a point where one must make a jump. It might be like sub-atomic particle physics, where the heart of it can only be reached through a leap from your thinking mind into another realm of perception. These are the highest realms of fire.

But there are "lower" realms, realms that are more common, part of every day life. As you walk along the street and you watch people coming towards you, most of them are not noticing you; they are in "a world of their own". They are thinking, dreaming, remembering, imagining. They are feeling, sensing and moving along partly in their animal bodies and partly in their imaginal bodies. Very few are actually thinking in the sense of working through a series of ideas – they are thinking in the sense of watching the drifting images that arise as they walk along.

Some of these images are water-based, and some are fire-based. Some of these images they could describe, if you stopped and asked them what had been in their heads a second before. But many of the images would be too diffuse for description – and of course many would be too private! Images have all sorts of density and range. When I say that fire is about imagination, I am not simply speaking of things you see in your imagination. I am speaking about a whole country, called Imagination. We shall explore it today through fire.

One more leap, and then we'll settle down a bit. This is an easier reach. I'll write the quotation on the board so you can remember it. Marcilio Ficino wrote, in his *Commentary on Plato's Phaedrus:* "Just as there are three main powers in fire – heat, light and fleeting subtlety – so there are three similar powers in the soul's essence – the power of life, of understanding and of desiring." Although he is not writing about astrology here, Ficino is telling us about the Sun, Jupiter and Mars. From here we can get into astrological fire directly.

THE FIERY RULERS

Astrological fire is differentiated in three ways: Aries fire, Leo fire and Sagittarius fire. Fire is first, in the sense that Aries is the first sign of the zodiacal cycle. But each of these fire signs come out of the water: Aries follows Pisces, Leo follows Cancer, and Sagittarius follows Scorpio. As water renders us helpless through our feelings, and this helplessness gives birth to our souls, so each water initiation leads to successive levels of fiery expression.

New life seems to leap into being from one day to the next. One day it is that indefinable time between two seasons, and the next day it is spring: Pisces into Aries. Life bursts into being and is given shape and form. Fire goes on into earth: Aries into Taurus.

The fire sign Leo follows the waters of Cancer as the child is born of the mother. From the waters of our common past we take the shape of our family's thread. We step into the light and take on our own name and our own destiny. When the child is born it must be cared for: Leo into Virgo.

The third stage of fire, Sagittarius, arises out of the waters of Scorpio. Out of this caldron of intense encounter, a light arises which gives meaning and purpose to life. And from this sense of meaning a demand is made. From Sagittarius to Capricorn, the vision must be manifested through work that is useful to the comm

Aries has, as its moving principle, Mars. Leo has, as its heart, the Sun. Sagittarius aims for the heights with its sky-god Jupiter leading the way. Before I speak about the fire signs, I want to look at Mars, Sun and Jupiter.

Let's look once again at this wonderful diagram.

fire	♈	♌	♐
ruler	♂	☉	♃
earth	♉	♍	♑
ruler	♀	☿	♄
air	♊	♎	♒
ruler	☿	♀	♄
water	♋	♏	♓
ruler	☽	♂	♃

You can see that both water and fire are ruled by Mars and Jupiter, with the Moon beginning the water story and the Sun at the heart of the fire story. I am not talking about the transpersonal rulers here. Both fire and water are informed by Mars and Jupiter. But fire has the Sun and water has the Moon at its centre. Earth and air are both ruled by different combinations of Venus, Mercury and Saturn. Both fire and water are moved by images, but the water images come from the past, arise from memories and ride on emotional waves. Fire images seem to arrive from the future, arise from potentials, and ride on excitement.

Let's go back to Ficino's comments on the three different powers of fire. One we might call the life force itself as it expresses itself through every one of us. This is the Sun. Another we might call the light of understanding, and that we call Jupiter. The third way fire expresses itself is through the heat of our desire nature, and that we call Mars. Both Venus and Mars operate from desire, but Venus has more to do with desires that reflect the soul life, and Mars with physical life, one's survival.

Mars

At a physical, microscopic level, Mars is 'sperm energy'. On the human scale it is the warrior, defending and protecting the king and therefore the kingdom. It is the fire which is heading for an act of creation, and it is the fire that defends and protects that which has been created. The first is the fire Mars and the second is the water Mars.

In the fiery Mars, we could say that the divine spark of the person to be created is carried in the sperm that gets to the egg. The egg contains endless memory, going back through woman after woman to the beginning of time and matter. This is released by the contact with the sperm. The past and the potential meet, and after a time of development, a brand new person is born into the world. But of course it is not that simple. The strands of memory in the egg contain sparks of creation, and the image in the sperm contains packets of memory too.

What I am interested in here is how Mars, as one of the personal planets, serves the life force. What is its role in our lives, and how do we begin to understand the images that drive it into action? Please be aware that I am not attempting to give you a textbook lesson on Mars. I am telling you what is most interesting to me about this planet: its connection to the imaginal plane, and how that informs its action. Now, what is Mars' action?

Audience: It wants something. It goes after it.

Audience: It acts on its desires. And I suppose that these desires must come from something imagined!

Audience: Yes, because when you desire something and you get it, you usually find out that it wasn't what you imagined.

Darby: Yes, desire, will and action arise out of Mars' imaginal plane. An impulse arises, and the impulse and the action often seem to be one. The image is pre-conscious. Mars' action is to act. Other things might get in the way of that impulse-into-action – feelings and thoughts and material obstacles – but the impulse to act comes from a perception of something desired. If we think of a very basic Mars, action becomes obvious. A man sees a woman. He desires her. He goes after her. He gets her. He loses interest in her. The image that propelled him forward dies with attainment. This can also happen to a woman, of course.

This is when desire, in the sense of moving purely from imagination, is dominating the field. Desire dominates most of us for some time in our lives, usually when we are young. Usually through experience and time it gets worn away, or integrated into other parts of ourselves. If one gets too hurt through experiences that bring disappointment, then it gets dulled, and so do one's vitality and one's connection to one's desire nature. Some people seem to keep their vitality all through their lives, while others begin to lose it quite young. When one is losing vitality, it can often be revived through physical activity – get the blood pumping and the imagination comes alive again. The imaginal fire of Mars always lights up images of something that must be won through some sort of action.

When we are young, Mars is the vital force that drives us towards food and comfort. It is very physical. We are hungry. We start to agitate, and then we yell! Sometimes I think that the particular sound each baby makes when it wants something could be matched up with various aspects to their Mars. Those yells are all geared to making the caretaker come *now*. But each one is so different. Sometimes they are powerful and compelling. Sometimes they are annoying and grinding in their sound. I wonder what dictates that? The aspects to Mars may tell you how people responded to your infant demands. And maybe the sign plus the aspects tell what sort of demand you made – the sound of your demand.

It certainly describes how you go after what you desire later in life. But we must distinguish it from Venus here. This Martial level of desire is connected directly to your life force. It is connected to action – it drives you forward, even if you get blocked before you have gone farther than an inch! Mars' action gets the blood moving and it demands you move forward. How you do that depends on the sign position and aspects to Mars.

Let's look at the rulership and exaltation of Mars. Mars rules Aries and, traditionally, Scorpio. It is in detriment in Libra, and from its early rulership it is also in detriment in Taurus. It is exalted in Capricorn. It is in fall in Cancer. So let's put together a statement about Mars with all of these ingredients. Mars expresses itself most naturally when it moves straight from impulse into action (Aries) or defence (Scorpio). Its vitality is checked when awareness of other people or aesthetic or ethical considerations oppose it (Libra), or when practical considerations, pleasure, expenditure or personal values (Taurus) slow it down. It acts from its imagined highest potential when it is working for the community in an ordered and considered way (Capricorn), and it is most hampered when feelings are involved (Cancer).

Audience: What is the difference, then, between the self-protection of Mars in Scorpio and Mars in Cancer?

Darby: Good question. It partly has to do with the frequency and indirectness with which Mars in Cancer reaches for its weapons – Cancer being ruled by the Moon. Mars in Scorpio moves seldom, but with great force. Feelings can interfere with action with Mars in Cancer. Feelings build up over time with Mars in Scorpio, and when people with this Mars act, they act with great clarity and power. When feelings are controlled for long periods of time, and then let loose, they have great destructive or creative power. When you see Mars in Cancer, look to the Moon to see what will activate this person's defence systems and also what will inspire their move to action.

Now, there is an interesting etymological trail embedded into the symbolic field around Mars. The main Greek antecedent of Mars is the brutish, ferocious god of the Greeks, Ares. But his name is connected to another word, *arete*. This word is associated with the innate, individuating, essential expression of a species. For instance, the *arete* of a horse would be its speed, and that of a bird might be its song. According to tradition, the *arete* of a man would be his reason. It is a word that denotes excellence, virtue, and skill. One who has it and uses it for the community is rewarded by the community.

In places and times where physical territory is fought over, the warrior is considered a most valuable member of his society. He both conquers others and brings back the spoils to enrich his group, and he defends his group from others. His excellence in doing this brings him honour and reward, and his ability to do this requires more than brute strength. This is why Athena was the councilor of heroes. Brute strength and courage wedded to wise council was unbeatable.

When you look at Mars in a chart, you are looking at something that exists to conquer for, defend and protect the territory that is you. It will do this according to its sign, house and aspects. It may do it crudely, but it will contain an image of excellence within it. Given the right circumstances and the right spiritual intent, this image of excellence may arise and take over, in time.

Audience: If it is trine Jupiter, does that mean it will do it with higher principles than if it is square the Sun, for instance?

Darby: If it is trine Jupiter, then it will go after what it "imagines" your heart's desire to be, with all your beliefs behind it. It will act with your truth and your principles on its side. If it is square the Sun, it will go into battle in such a way that you feel unprotected and beleaguered, but it does not mean you don't passionately approve of its fight.

Jung said that Mars is the planet of individuation, and that is interesting for a number of reasons. He said, "Astrologically Mars characterises the instinctual and affective nature of man. The subjugation and transformation of this nature seems to be the theme of the alchemical opus." Many of you know that I am fascinated with the very ancient notion of "navigating desire". There is no way round it: if you are dominated by your desire nature, you have no autonomy or freedom, no true individuality. If you suppress your desire nature, you lose your vitality and your creativity. Mars' journey from loutishness to excellence depends not on killing the dragon, but on riding it on behalf of something greater than yourself. But to get there takes time.

When you are working with Mars in charts, you are seeing the sort of things that will activate desire (the sign), and the domain that will be lit up by this desire (the house), and the obstacles and assistances you will have from other quarters of yourself or your environment (the aspects). But what you won't see from the chart is whether this person is navigating or being swept along by inner or outer circumstances.

Audience: While you have been speaking, I have been remembering something that happened recently, and I wonder if my husband is engaged in some sort of private battle with himself. He has Mars conjunct Uranus in Gemini in the 12th house – he's a double Cancerian. He sometimes says things that are so incredibly hurtful or tactless or shocking that people's jaws drop, literally. He is not a cruel man – in fact, he is very kind – but it's as if he just gets taken over suddenly, and he comes out with things! Recently I went at him for something he said to one of his nephews, and he got upset and said, "I do try now, can't you see that? Sometimes I stop myself in time, but that time it just got out." Because Mars is in the 12th I didn't know that he was really struggling with it – he always acted as if he felt completely justified in saying outrageous things. He wouldn't talk about it much, but later he said he had known he would "get possessed by a smart-Alick". It's only recently that he has begun to really pay attention to it. I have noticed he is getting more mellow. I hadn't known he was working at it.

Audience: I'm not sure I like the idea of getting too much control over my desires. Sometimes desires sweep you along to all sorts of amazing things.

Darby: Those who are later able to govern themselves have usually had a time of being swept here and there by their desires for years. Those who have suppressed them for years on end find it even harder to find their own unique place, their own self, than do those who have been swept into all sorts of messy but fertile experiences.

The Sun

The Sun is the heart of the fire realm and contains the image at the centre of your heart. When you meditate on the Sun, when you image yourself through your Sun, you reach for the life-giving spark that both circumscribes you and connects you to all life. In *Revelation* it says, "God hands you a white stone, and that's your name." That "name", that "signature" is encoded in your Sun.

Henry Corbin says that each thing has its signature, and that signature is the fire at the heart of it. Your Sun is the clue to that. This signature is the secret of your heart's desire. So when your Sun is in Aries, Leo or Sagittarius, perhaps it is easier to know and to feel your signature directly. There is no other element through which the fire has to be translated. This is why these signs are noted to be, in general, positive, outgoing, enthusiastic, but also arrogant, foolhardy, reckless. You feel alive when you are in touch with the essential part of yourself – and at the heart of a fire Sun, the image burns bright. Other planets might block the expression of this essence, so that you may not be able to act from it simply and clearly. They may indicate how you lose touch with it. Many people struggle with their sense of identity, and when they come to us, as astrologers, they say things like, "I want to take time to find myself." Finding oneself may mean clearing a pathway to the image that burns at the heart of the Sun.

Audience: Couldn't you use active imagination to get someone to find this place you are talking about?

Darby: Most certainly you could. Techniques of active imagination are good for getting people in touch with any planet in fire. But I do think we should be careful when releasing other people's imaginations – we must know what we are playing with here. Remember that fire is dangerous when not handled wisely, and many people play with imagination now in ways that are deeply irresponsible. There is immense power in images, because behind all images is the spiritual realm, where infinite possibilities dwell. We are very experimental these days, and that is exciting, but a lot of times we don't know we are experimenting with dangerous elements, and so people get burned. Mess around with memory and you are in the realm of water and water's dangers. Play with imagination and you are in the world of fire. Put up a sign when you do this: Handle With Care.

Audience: I think leaving the world of the imagination and coming back into the present must be one of the most important parts of any ritual.

Darby: Yes, I think so, too. And I also think that using active imagination to reach the fire in one's Sun is a good way to reconnect with your own centre. In my early years in London I worked with someone who was experienced in imaginative techniques, and we did workshops in Hampstead using only active imagination to teach the basics of astrology. It was very exciting, but from that I realised that intellectual input was absolutely necessary when teaching astrology. People could become consumed by the images that arose in them, and with no tradition and no intellectual container, they had no idea what to do with those images. Astrology could not really be learned simply through accessing the images at the heart of the symbols. We had to bring the images into the denser realms of thought and practise and emotional experience. Later Melanie [Reinhart] and I ran a summer school for a few years, and we combined imagination and intellect in our teaching, which worked to great effect.

In the break, you might like to experiment with each other in this way: Sit across from each other and decide who will go first – the other person attends and reflects, the Moon to your Sun. Draw the symbol for the Sun on paper, in the sand or however you devise, and gaze at it for a period of time until your eyes are ready to close. They will naturally close as the images start to rise inside. Watch the image for a time, and then let your senses begin to pull you back to the external world again. You don't have to get complicated, just watch for a time and then return. Let your eyes open and look at the Sun symbol again, move your body around a bit, and make contact with your "attendant". The whole point of the Sun is that it shines, so express the image to the other person. The words and the response are part of it, because they bring the image into being. The central fire radiates warmth to you, and you radiate it to others. And, as we just said, close the experiment carefully; leave the circle of your ritual with care and attention. Don't do any active imagination techniques with people you don't like or trust. I think that is always important.

Audience: You used the word "desire" with both Mars and the Sun. You differentiate them by saying "the heart's desire" when you speak about the Sun. I would like to know more about what you mean.

Darby: When I say that the Sun carries the image of the heart's desire, I am saying something about personal destiny. To achieve your destiny, you have to move from stage to stage – your character has to be forged through various experiences so that it is fit to carry the fire in your heart into the world in whatever way it is "written" in your heart. Mars "desires" certain things and people and experiences which it "imagines" will give you the fulfillment of your destiny. Whether it "imagines" correctly – in other words, whether the things you desire and get actually bring you closer to shining your light in a way that deeply satisfies you – depends on other things!

Audience: Such as aspects between Mars and the other planets?

Darby: Yes. But also something else. I think we have to learn to navigate desire at some point in our lives, especially the desires that arise from the imagined potential in things. Remember Jung's description of Mars as the individuating principle. Unless one can bring consciousness and self-direction to one's desire nature, one cannot claim any true freedom or autonomy. The desire of the heart, to go back to the Sun, is something directly linked to one's spiritual connection to the light – a "desire" of the spirit, not the body and its appetites.

Audience: What about the Sun representing the father?

Darby: Yes, I think that is very strange and wonderful. You are born in a particular month along with everyone else who is born that month. All of you have the same Sun-signs, and yet by sign and house and aspect you can definitely describe the father of your client in such a way that he is recognised by your client, and often with breathtaking accuracy. You see your client's sister three weeks later, and her Sun and its aspects are different, and again you describe her father clearly. How can this be? We can only go to the realms of the imagination to find any clues as to why this might be. One day scientists may find explanations that satisfy the requirements of other levels of reason.

If you think of the Sun as the carrier of your "signature", that "name" written deep in the core of your being, something will have to activate it once you are out of the womb and into the sunlight. Many pre-industrial cultures have rituals for taking the infant out of the dwelling where it was born and into the sun-light. Some wait weeks to do this; others do it quite soon after birth. You might say that the seed of your father carries the image of the Sun, but it needs the touch of your father to activate it naturally. After that, each touch of your father – or any substitute it can find, if the seed-father is not there – reinforces it until it is active on its own and "runs by itself".

Audience: When?

Darby: I don't know, really, but I imagine that it must be after the age of seven. The Sun has returned to itself seven times and this very sacred number has initiation ceremonies attached to it all over the world.

Audience: Even your Catholic Church.

Darby: Yes! Even "my" Catholic Church! We spoke about that in the Moon seminars, because the first progressed lunar square occurs around seven years old, and through this we get our first clear angle on ourselves. But the Sun has also completed seven circuits of the zodiac by age seven. A sense of identity is awakened at this point. The Sun and the Moon are always in relation to each other. So wherever your Sun is, it will be connected to your Moon, if not directly by aspect, by lunar phase, certainly. The Moon will describe the emotional field through which you express your Sun, no matter what their relationship.

Fire signs who have lost their vision droop visibly. An Aries who doesn't know where he or she is heading, a Leo who cannot find a proper stage, and a Sagittarius who has lost the sense of meaning, lose their vitality. Fire signs have to be able to imagine possibilities, to be in contact with the next potential. Then the fire burns through them.

Let's see what more we can learn about the Sun from looking at the fact that it rules Leo and is in the sign of its detriment in Aquarius. It is exalted in Aries and in fall in Libra. What do you think about that?

Audience: Its detriment and fall are both in air signs. That is odd, because you would think that fire and air are compatible.

Audience: I am a Libra, and I can understand it being in fall there. It's that need for balance – it seems to slow everything down so much. If we had two Suns in the solar system, it would be fine – then we could put our own Sun on one side and the other person's Sun on the other side of the scale and it would feel fine.

Darby: It would? That's an interesting notion. It is thought-provoking that the Sun is not given great marks in two of the air signs. The Sun is exalted in Aries, and that tells us that personal destiny is fulfilled when one's action is behind one's heart's desire. The fall in Libra says that when fulfilling the heart's desire, if one's destiny depends on someone else, or on perfectly proportioned circumstances, that is not such a happy condition. The Sun rules Leo, and that says that, to fulfill one's personal destiny, one must follow one's heart's desire. The Sun's detriment in Aquarius tells us that fulfilling one's destiny does not depend on the world being an ideal place where everyone operates from the right principles.

It is easier to feel as though you are fulfilling your destiny when your Sun is in fire signs, and especially if the Sun is unimpeded by other planets. But always remember that life is endlessly mysterious, and we are each part of something bigger than we can ever know. It is a wonderful thing to feel as though you are fulfilling what was "intended" for you. It feels so good when you are connected to the fire in your heart, and doing things that express this fire. But this is a luxury not given to everyone. Many people go through life not knowing what they are "intended" for, and not having a sense of destiny. This does not make them any less valuable than those who do feel destined. People who feel destined can be full of qualities that are less than admirable, and all in the service of this "imagined" destiny. Planets in rulership and exaltation work well according to their nature. But because you have a great sword, and you know where you are going, that doesn't mean you are a fine person full of compassion and patience and humour. These are things you develop through a lifetime of experiences, and they are probably not written in the planets and aspects of your chart. The planets and aspects tell you about the journey that is you. What you do with it is a secret deeper than our knowing.

Jupiter

Let me say something about Jupiter here. Later in the day we will talk about aspects to these fire planets. Now I simply want to set the stage.

Audience: Now we know where your fire planets are.

Darby: And you're right! If the Sun is the carrier of the spark of light that connects you to the whole through your personal destiny – your place within the body of humankind – and Mars carries the spark into action through images that translate as desire, then what is Jupiter?

Audience: Jupiter expands your world. You are given opportunities through Jupiter that open you out to things beyond your own familiar territory.

Darby: That's nice. I once had a conversation about that with a Jungian analyst in Zurich, about ten years ago. She was also an astrologer. She said, in the course of our conversation, "Whenever I get stuck with someone when I am doing their chart, I look to Jupiter and I start talking about it. It always opens things up again. I get to their better selves that way." I brought it into my mental Jupiter-Saturn file. I was working on Jupiter and Saturn at the time, and beginning to see them as socialising planets. I was discovering them describing the energies that stood between the personal and the collective – and I identified them with community life.

The personal planets describe one's very personal needs and possibilities. I was exploring how the transpersonal planets, Uranus, Neptune, and Pluto, are the mind, feelings and survival instinct of what I call the "body of mankind". They are so far beyond the personal that they become the carrier of something we call esoteric. I was looking at Jupiter and Saturn as the middle ground, the realm of faith and discipline that one develops in relation to a community. I was exploring shared beliefs and laws in community life.

Jupiter is the fire that connects you to the larger picture, wherever you start from. It is the planet that functions as the explorer, but it is also the priest in you. In a culture where religion binds people together, it may be the way in which you see the function of the priest in your community. In a non-religious culture it becomes personalised, and so we find people who passionately believe their own version of the truth to be universal. Religion tries to contain the Jupiterian access to the archetypal world. At best, it tries to channel that intuition of something beyond our ordinary senses into personal and collective rituals that will bind the community together.

Audience: Doesn't Jupiter describe one's moral stance, too?

Darby: Yes, it does, but not what you do about it. Aspects to your Jupiter will show how you live that moral stance. The Sun carries the image of your true self, your "signature", your "name" in the esoteric sense. Your Mars carries the image of action on behalf of this self, and Jupiter is...

Audience: ...Your potential self. It has potential to expand; it is your future self.

Darby: Yes, in some ways it is just that! I think you imagine yourself in your best light through your Jupiter placement, and sometimes that can be the problem. You imagine yourself as whole and completely in tune with the perfect unfolding of creation through your Jupiter function. But do you act according to this picture? Others in the community will decide that. But it's always where you are unfolding towards some potential image of completeness, and you identify with it because it feels good!

Audience: But Jupiter is about excess and inflation, too.

Darby: It certainly is. It is where our imagination of our own wholeness and truth can get out of proportion. We "see" the truth through our Jupiter, and unless we are careful, we really believe that our truth is The Truth; and that leads to all sorts of madness. Isn't it interesting that it was the planet of moderation and temperance in the Renaissance?

Audience: But that was a more religious society. Arrogance was only for the rich and privileged and those connected with the Church! I wonder if the lack of religious containers coincides with the worship of travel for travel's sake, and tourism, and the worship of sport?

Darby: Interesting observation. If I keep moving, I might find a sense of meaning, purpose and connection to the universe?
     Jupiter is the pattern recognition faculty in ourselves. Jupiter is where we imagine the patterns that make life meaningful for us. In Jupiter's fire there is an image of wholeness, an image that draws one onwards towards a feeling of purpose and truth. One finds the truth for oneself through the sign Jupiter tenants. Both Sagittarius and Pisces claim its rulership, although Pisces has been veering towards Neptune since its discovery, and we can certainly see how Pisces is connected to the mysteries of Neptune's realm. Still, it's important to remember that Jupiter is the ancient ruler of Pisces, and it still works beautifully in Pisces' world and has a lot to tell us about a Jupiter that we have perhaps forgotten. Both Gemini and Virgo are places of detriment for Jupiter. These are both Mercury-ruled signs, and perhaps this is telling us that the ephemeral world of Mercury is not an easy

place to find patterns of meanings. Jupiter in these two signs can get lost in the trivia and details of life, or make meaning out of everything.

Jupiter is exalted in Cancer and in fall in Capricorn. Fire and water are connected with Jupiter's exaltation in Cancer. Nature is abundance. Jupiter's exaltation in Cancer tells us something profound about the search for meaning. It says that, no matter where your Jupiter is, no matter what house and sign, your search for spiritual meaning and your wish for "good fortune" can only bring nourishment if they are connected to the simple and common things. If the vision you follow ultimately cuts you off from caring and tending the small, the old and the familiar, then it will shrivel you up, rather than expand your life. "Jupiter is exalted in Cancer" is nearly an astrological *Haiku* – the universal in the particular in one small phrase. It is like Wittgenstein's "the world is all that is the case". Jupiter's exaltation in Cancer is astrological code for half of everything we ever need to know. Saturn's exaltation in Libra is the code for all the rest.

Jupiter's fall in Capricorn has its simple message too: you can't get to heaven by building churches. It tells us that no matter what you do for yourself, others or the community at large, unless it is infused with your passion, unless it has meaning for you in the sense of feeling the heat of it in your imagination, then it will not give you the "good fortune" of joy.

Audience: Perhaps those with Jupiter in Capricorn have to work to find confidence and joy.

Darby: Perhaps. You can see why Jupiter is equated with confidence, because when you imagine that your life has meaning how can you not have confidence? But when you imagine your life has a "special meaning", then we are back in Jupiter's temptation towards arrogance. Arrogance isolates you from others in your community, and that isolation brings you down in the end. The Greeks called it *hubris,* and it meant being too identi-fied with the gods, but it may also be the price for setting yourself apart through your "important work".

These are the traps for those who identify too closely with Jupiter. When the priest identifies with his vision of God, he be-comes mad. When we identify with our vision too closely, we be-gin to say things like, "I have very important work to do." Much of religious training is focused on dealing with this, because it is such a common problem with those who have been "called" to their work. In daily life we don't have formalised rituals, but informal ones arise in each community to deal with those who take themselves too seriously. Some of these are helpful to the community, but sometimes they are destructive to individuality and creativity too.

It seems as though we do need a context for Jupiter. Like Sat-urn, it is not meant to be appropriated by the ego; it belongs to a wider consciousness. It is our ticket to "out there", and it opens our imagination to adventures that lure us by their promise: Fol-low me and you will understand the meaning of life. If your Ju-piter is strong then life is an adventure, but you can identify so strongly with it that you think you know the meaning of life, and that does bring *hubris* along with it. Religion used to "channel" our Jupiterian impulses when we gave them away to our priests and rabbis. Fewer of us do that now, and so a little knowledge becomes a dangerous thing! But I guess there is a fail-safe within Jupiter's field – get too high on yourself and you come down. On the other hand, ignore the call to adventure, and you lose hope and faith in life's infinite possibilities and end up unlived. Per-haps Jupiter's adventurousness and excess do lead to temper-ance and moderation after all. And so the traveler gets wise in the end.

If I have Jupiter in fire, then I believe simply because I be-lieve. If it is in Aries, my action and my belief are one. If it is in Leo, then I believe in myself when I am in the midst of creation.

In Sagittarius I am propelled forward into the future by my beliefs – I believe in the future and I follow it as it unfolds. The images of the unfolding potential speak directly through Jupiter in
fire. Jupiter in fire is great for "knowing" the meaning, purpose,
and pattern of things because it taps into the spiritual potential
of things. However, it must be controlled, and unless this vision
takes in the commonality of creatureness, it goes awry. Visionaries who forget the range of people who are being affected by
their actions are generally destructive.

Audience: Won't you say something about Jupiter in the other
elements?

Darby: Right now I would like to talk about the fire signs, Aries, Leo and Sagittarius. I'll say something about the planets in
these signs as I go along. After that I'll come back to Mars, Sun
and Jupiter, and touch on their action in the other elements. But
remember, I am doing seminars on each of the elements, and so,
in the end, we will get round to saying something about the all of
the planets in all of the signs, one way or another.

There is something I have been thinking about for a while,
and I would like to mention it here. Jupiter describes the place
where you will be most confident, most "full" of yourself, and I
think it also describe the fantasy you have of yourself as a sexual
being. I think it describes the image you have of yourself as the
Lover (but not the Beloved). I mean the positive image that you
carry, in spite of whatever contrary evidence you might collect
on your way!

If you think of Jupiter's mythic ancestor, Zeus, then you can
see how this might be true. I started checking this notion with
some of my friends, and I said to one of them, "But people will
rarely be honest about their sexual fantasies of themselves as
lovers." She answered, "Well, I have Jupiter in Gemini in the 1st
house, so I will. It is square my Sun in Pisces and opposing my

THE FIERY RULERS   149

Mars in Sagittarius, and I think the two sexiest men I have ever seen are Harpo Marx and Billy Wilder." I said, "But Harpo Marx was silent!" And she said, "Not to a Pisces, he wasn't. He was brilliant at communication. And Billy Wider is a hugely expressive, zany, very funny man." Thinking of it now, I should have asked her if she saw herself as a zany, entertaining lover. Venus and Mars will tell you about your physical love life – but Jupiter may tell you about your fantasy love life!

Don't you think this would be an interesting avenue for research? However, it might be hard to get the truth of people's fantasies of themselves out in the open. We must always remember that Jupiter rules Pisces, underneath the broader sweep of Neptune's sway, and so there is a secret side of it, too.

ARIES

In the Aries expression of fire, the impulse which arises from the imagined potential is quick and sharp. Often the image itself is barely conscious. Aries seems to act so quickly on its impulses that it may seem as if the image and the impulse rise together. "Why did you do that?" you ask your Aries friend or client. There is always an imagined outcome fueling the impulse, but the answer is often contained in the end product of the impulse. The spark is lit and the flame and the person are one. This is why people with planets in Aries seem so willful. The spark ignites the will, and the will moves the person forward to achieve something, arrive somewhere, initiate something. Of course, there are many times when forward movement is impaired – planets in Aries are not always trine and sextile other planets! When the impulse arises and it is blocked by another equally powerful energy, then there is frustration, as there is with any planet that is blocked.

With Aries energy, if the blockage goes on for too long, then the impulse dies. It needs movement to keep it alive. It requires immediate action, and of course that is not always possible. Impulses arise and are often crushed – it is part of daily life, and this is particularly acute for people with planets in Aries. If enough of the sparks become fires – in other words, if enough of them get translated into action which results in creation – then the person feels alive and vital. If too many of them are blocked, and do not get translated into action which has results, then the person loses vitality and rattles around knocking the furniture over.

Planets in the 1st house

The 1st house is associated with Aries. It describes the way our unconscious behaviour and appearance make a mark on our world. We are always aware of how others impact on us, but we are so often unaware of how we impact on others. The Ascendant describes the image presented by the personality through which we express ourselves. It is an image, but often we grow more and more like that image as we get older. It seems to function as an ideal for personality development. The sign on the cusp of the 1st house, the Ascendant, points to a planet, usually somewhere else. This planet gives the inner motivation that drives the image. For example, Aries rising will instinctively rise to challenges, and others will experience them, generally, as tough, or feisty, or aggressive. But Mars will tell you what activates the instinct to fight or challenge the world. In the 7th house, it will usually be other people. In the 9th house, it might be the image of travel or education that activates the instinct to leap into action. Taurus rising people instinctively convey security, but someone with Venus in Cancer square Mars in Aries may create an image of emotional security while desiring action and challenge. Most people are motivated by things they are not aware of, and often their desires go in other directions, too, so it can get confusing.

When there are planets conjunct the Ascendant, then they very much colour your instinctive approach to life. Saturn on the Ascendant will stiffen the reactions a bit, no matter what sign it is in. You have to get past it, to find what is really driving the personality. So, for example, if Venus is on the Ascendant in Aries, and Mars is in Capricorn in the 10th, you might be distracted by Venus for a time before you see that this person is really driven by the need to master and accomplish something recognisably useful for their world.

Sometimes we have another sign in addition to the rising sign in the 1st house, and planets in that sign, too. And so we experience the initial impression, and then we see different layers as we go along. Pisces rising will come in like a lamb, but if Mars is in Aries in the 1st, you will notice that it doesn't take much to get this person lit up with inspiration or with anger, once a challenge is offered through an exciting image, this Pisces rising becomes a warrior.

Planets in Aries

Aries is ruled by Mars. We have looked at Mars as action and will and desire. It is the warrior of the Sun, isn't it? It fights for and defends the kingdom in any way it can. You might say that, if it is well-aspected, then it has been trained by good teachers. The important thing to remember is that its nature is to fight on be-half of the Sun. But it is does not always fight wisely. Most of us develop wisdom from all our foolish mistakes. Of course, there are those who never develop much wisdom no matter how many mistakes they make, but most of us do learn a bit as we go along – we get wiser where we have been most unwise. It is your Mars that crashes you into the walls that bruise your bones, but it is this very same Mars which is always rushing out to protect and defend your life force. No matter where Mars is in your chart, no matter what sign, what house and how aspected, it will always express itself crudely some of the time.

Audience: "How did you get so wise?" they said to the old man who always sat under the tree. "Good judgement," he said. "How did you get such good judgement?" they said. "Good experi-ence," he said. "How did you get all that good experience?" they asked. "Bad judgement!" he said.

Darby: Wonderful! Probably it is your Mars that drives you to the sorts of experiences that this is talking about. By nature, Mars points to the most unredeemed and unregenerated part of yourself. You cannot civilise it completely. You can put Saturn on it, but it will break out of that jail, commit a crime, and then go back in. In terms of the person's life force, it is in its nature to fight. So it is not hold-downable. Mars' action ends when you breathe your last. Nobody can suppress Mars. You can stop it for a time, you can pervert it, but it keeps fighting. That is its nature. It is there to serve the Sun by its weapons, and it will use them in one way or another until the last. It may be crude in its expression, but its motive is pure and simple. It is driven by the image of its Sun's essential being and its aim is to keep the king alive long enough so that, given the right circumstances, it will fulfill its essential being or purpose.

With **Mars in Aries**, then, the drive is clear – when the person goes after something, it is obvious what the intention is. With Mars in Aries, the object of desire is not usually far away in time; it is within striking distance. If it becomes something that takes much longer than expected, then it gets pretty grueling, and there has to be a pretty strong Saturn somewhere to get that Mars up again and again. Sometimes Jupiter can do it too, by inflaming Mars with vision again, after it has collapsed.

Mars will express its crude side if it is in Aries, in that it will suddenly do something blatantly selfish. In an otherwise gentle nature, this is usually a shock for those around it, if not to itself. This is a very direct Mars. No matter how complex and confusing other sides of the personality may be, this Mars cuts through it all and leaps into life with great excitement, aiming straight for whatever has turned it on. It is lit by bright daring people, yet oddly enough, it often attracts more passive natures for long-term relationships.

Now, let's look at **the Sun in Aries**. It is here in its sign of exaltation. The Sun shines with a happy light in Aries. It shines with passion and energy. The king is lit up when travelling through the kingdom of Mars. Now, here is an interesting thing about this Sun. It seems to me that the Sun follows Mars in the youth of Sun in Aries – the "heart's desire" is to get what it wants, here and now! But I have known many Aries who, having gone through some sort of spiritual crisis at some point in their lives, then seem to gather their Mars' energy, their desire nature, into the service of something more than their own satisfaction. Things are achieved through will and passion and energy, and it is very exciting. Of course, the excitement does not last, and the Sun has to send Mars out on scouting trips to find new challenges. Mars' position and aspects will say what sort of images Mars brings back. It usually brings back several possibilities, before the Aries central Sun fire is lit up with that energising and beloved "sense of destiny".

Audience: What about if the Sun is in Aries, but Mars is in Cancer conjunct Saturn in Cancer, and both are squaring the Sun? Is the Sun happy then?

Darby: You are really throwing things at me here, aren't you? Could we be in Mars' country, by any chance? All right; Mars and its aspects do not take away from the fact that the Sun is in its sign of exaltation. But in the case you offer, it is squared by Mars in its sign of fall, and Saturn in its sign of detriment! Pretty powerful stuff. So the Sun seeks to initiate activity – its aim is to get things moving, to venture out, be at the head of the wagon train. It doesn't have to be the only one there – that is a fallacy, that Aries wants to be first and alone of the first. Aries wants to be in the first team, part of the group that goes out ahead of the others. Aries is not particularly drawn to loneliness, as some of the other signs might be.

Now, here – with Mars and Saturn struggling in territories far from home, both in the realm of the Moon – the Aries Sun may have to battle with obstacles that are not natural for a warrior king. Its warrior is clearing up the swamps, feeding the people, rebuilding the dwellings and dealing with the emotions of his household staff. In other words, this Aries Sun may have to battle with things that seem to get in the way of letting the person get off to their "true" battle. And that true battle is a vision they carry in their heart, which is often pre-verbal and often imageless. It is a vision which drives the person forward, but it may only be seen by those who look closely, rarely by the one who has it. The courage and the will to strive out are there, but the battleground in this case, is often more swampy than the king and even the warrior, would wish. Of course, some of the most noble battles are won in the most private parts of our lives. Sun in Aries is usually as shining and bright at ninety as it was at fifteen. Even though the battles may have been in unexpected territories, a warrior is still a warrior, and nothing seems to dim that!

Audience: I have **Venus in Aries**, and I know that is supposed to be "in detriment". But I'm not sure why it is bad – I don't think I am selfish with my loving.

Darby: You have to admit, with Venus in Aries, that you might say that! But perhaps this notion of detriment must be examined more closely. We'll do that one day. For now, let me say that Venus in Aries does seem to have quite a good time loving. I don't know that it is a problem for the one who has it, though it can be for those who love the one who has it. Venus in Aries is in Mars' domain. So she puts on a gleaming helmet and rushes off looking for love. She is excited by the very thought of love! She loves loving. Her nature is to rush into love without thought, and she does that for awhile, at least in her youth. She carries weapons and uses them wildly at first, and over time she gains skill. Depending on other things, she is capable of fidelity, but her heart will leap at the sight of beauty all through life.

Venus is in detriment in Aries because the deepest satisfaction in love, the deepest nourishment, comes from those plants and trees with the deepest roots. Trees which are two hundred and fifty years old give us a sense of security and images of continuity that feed our very souls. They have a beauty of symmetry and grace that touches something eternal in us. Love that has been seasoned for fifty years, and still nourishes, satisfies one of our deepest needs. Venus in Aries does not do that naturally – and so we say it is in detriment. The woman who has Venus in Aries may bring the dead back to life with her loving. The man with Venus in Aries may spark his beloved to her greatest creative passion. That it is in detriment simply says that it is operating in ways that oppose its most natural nature – that's all.

Audience: My client on Friday had Venus in Aries square Mars in Cancer. She said that she fell in love with men who were "domesticated", as she put it, because she always saw a spark of adventure that they had not lived out yet. She brought it out of them, but then she got bored "doing all the work", as she put it.

Darby: The very hard part of this work, the work we do as psychological astrologers, is how to truly recognise and help our clients recognise that we are all of our planets. Your client's "warrior" fights for security (and fights security). This is the territory in which her "warrior princess" finds love and inspiration. I have a client with Venus in Aries opposite Mars in Libra. He is very smart, and can see how he plays out this "absurd dance", as he calls it. He gets enormously excited by inspired, energetic women, and then finds himself passive and walked over by them. We work together to find images which will activate his own Venus self, and he has had fun with that. But last time he said, "I just wonder if a huge part of me doesn't rather enjoy the indolent pleasure of watching her throw the flowers I have just given her into the fire because, she says, I gave them to her for the wrong reasons."

Audience: What about **the Moon in Aries**?

Darby: The image of the Amazon or warrior queen must be contained in the shape of this Moon, though it will depend on where Mars is in the chart. Always remember to look at Mars by sign and position and aspects when you are looking at planets in Aries. The Moon here takes its impulses from its brave, reckless, proactive ancestresses, and so it has to be on the move, on its way to conquering the next hill or mountain or planet to keep its emotions sparking. If the mother has provided an image of courage and prowess, then Moon in Aries enjoys its conquests. I know a lot of people with Moon in Aries opposite Neptune in Libra, and that is harder, because there is an early confusion about appropriate behaviour. Direct action towards self-gratification and lingering guilt accompany each other. If one can see that others will benefit from one's impulses, then that feels better. The Moon in Aries' cruder impulses will be refined in Neptune's misty landscape.

Now, what about **Saturn in Aries**, which is in detriment? That is also a very close connection, though not a famously comfortable one. Saturn is in Aries right now, and as there are several of you in the room who are in the middle of your Saturn return, let me say something about that too.

The thing I notice about people with Saturn in Aries is that their courage and their fears lead them into situations where they have to learn "the hard way". Their battles are with their wills. They are halted in their forward drive in such a way that they can feel as if the world is against them, and yet they have to go on. There is the very odd juxtaposition that Saturn is in detriment in Aries and Mars is exalted in Capricorn. Inner limitations seem to be more difficult to a warrior than outer limitations, which strengthen a warrior. When Saturn is moving through Mars' domain he shuts down all the pubs because the nightly fighting disturbs the community. When Mars travels through Saturn's domain he opens schools for martial arts, gets some action going, stirs up the blood, challenging the rules in such a way that they have to be re-examined or renovated. When you see Saturn in Aries, look to Mars to see what sort of battles are fought in the name of the Sun, and then look to the house where Saturn is to see what this person is trying to safeguard here.

For example, a man with Saturn in Aries in the 5th and Mars in Pisces in the 4th, with Sun in Capricorn, is building an empire to perpetuate the myth of his family name, and he sees himself as doing this in great part for his children. Saturn in Aries bats its head against walls to learn what is appropriate and what is not within the structure of the community. During this man's Saturn return he is finding out how much his children will be controlled by his desire that they be safe. The outlaw streak in Saturn in Aries means that he and his children vie over who is making and who is breaking the rules now. His son just joined an expedition going to the Antarctic. His father sees this as deeply unsafe, but admires him enormously, too. He has to let his son go. And he has to continue to work to fight to make him safe at some future point. He imagines the worst, if he doesn't work very hard: Saturn in Aries.

Those of you who are in the eighteen-month period of your Saturn return: keep track of your desires. Those of you who can, begin to ride with your Mars, rather than being always ridden by it. Get to know the part of yourself that defends your desires with all its power because it feels so threatened by those who do not support what you want. The house which Saturn tenants is what you are defending. Mars is the way you are defending it. Pay attention. Bring the light of your consciousness to this, because otherwise the frustration of wanting and not getting what you want in the way you want it can be incredibly time-consuming and upsetting. Go after what you want, but be prepared to give it up at the same time. Begin to navigate your desires. Ride that edge and you'll find yourself on a new adventure.

Now let's speak about Jupiter. **Jupiter in Aries** is in Mars' territory, and so it believes what it believes with passion and fervour, and it acts instinctively on its beliefs. It rushes headlong into action with its banners flying. It fires up the environment with its beliefs, but it may be so full of conviction that it rouses others to instinctively oppose it. Jupiter in Aries either fires others to reaction, or it activates the warrior in others. Its beliefs are so personal, so fierce and fuelled with a lot of personal need – the need to be honoured for the courage of its convictions.

If you hold beliefs other than those which someone with Jupiter in Aries holds, it is almost impossible for the one with this position to understand and tolerate your position. It is wonderfully brave and full of good intentions and, given the opportunity, will leap to the challenges offered. The slow grinding of earthtime reality can teach it wisdom in action, but it can also dampen its ardour again and again. Yet you can always get it active again by lobbing philosophical grenades into its courtyard.

Audience: What about **Chiron in Aries**?

Darby: I see Chiron as something you needed to learn about when you were young, but nobody knew that they should teach it to you. It is not like Saturn, which describes an imbalance in your nature that is inherent, and then reinforced by your early conditioning. Chiron seems to describe a gap between your earth self and your spirit self. The sign and house and aspects show you where you feel the gap. This place hurts, and so you try to heal it, to bridge the gap, and this takes you on a journey. You have all read Melanie's book on Chiron, and you have worked with her on it, so I am sure you have quite a good sense of this place in yourselves. I'll just say one or two things I have personally noticed.

Chiron in Aries is the very opposite of Mars in Aries, in a sense. With Mars in Aries, rising images move you to action that increases the excitement, stirs the blood and pushes you to one or another edge. Through that you feel alive. With Chiron in Aries, the images that move you bring you to the gap between your animal body and your spirit self. That is the place of hurt, of the wound. You feel the power of the image that arises, but it activates an awareness of impotence in the face of something unfixable. You have to act, you have to move, but you don't know how to. You could say that your parents didn't teach you to run properly or to jump off the swing. You have to dare, but daring opens the wound for you. You can't stop it because wherever Chiron is, you have to do it; you can't not do it. In doing it, the wound opens, and it is the wound of incarnation. Fire can know that, just by being incarnated, there is a distortion, there is a woundedness, and the very nature of life is cure. The cure, when Chiron is in fire, lies in the imagination. It is the way you are reacting to the images that demand courage, which constellates the feeling of helplessness in your life.

Audience: My father is a Sagittarian, and he has Chiron in Aries. He never had the faith to change his job. My mother has a Sun-Mars conjunction, and whenever a job offer came in, she would say, "Go for it!" But he never dared. He didn't have faith in his ability. He just stayed with the same job. He has Venus in Sagittarius and Sun square Uranus, but he lived his whole life with this one job. Others would come up, and Mum would urge him to try them out, but he just didn't dare.

Darby: With Chiron we notice the people who are doing the things we can't do, and that keeps our own wound active.

Audience: He is dismissive of young kids rising up in the world now. He says, "Oh, it's all show biz!" about someone who is taking chances and putting everything into a new enterprise. We were in the bar, and I got angry and said, "Oh, Dad, you're saying that just because you were a failure." He just sat there and glowered, and said, "It's no sin to be mediocre."

Darby: Well, that's interesting. Do you know Quentin Crisp? He once said, in a television interview, "Just be what you are. If you are mediocre, then be absolutely mediocre. Be so mediocre that everyone who knows you recognises you through your perfect mediocrity. Let it become your style." Am I right in thinking he is a Sagittarian? That's a fire sign being mediocre!

And your father is a Sagittarian! But I do think that Chiron in Aries has the problem that you are speaking about. "If I move with this image and take a chance, I will be wiped out." Or it could also be that the image of movement has something in it that stops the movement. Chiron in fire is always about a wounded imagination. The very nature of the image stops the forward movement into action. Overcoming the dark and frightening image takes what we call courage. Contrast this with Saturn in Aries, where the warnings of danger contained in the image are ignored. I knew someone very well with Saturn in Aries, and he was famously brave. Once I asked him about his courage, and he said mostly it wasn't real courage, because he never really saw the danger in his acts as a more imaginative person might. He told me about a time when he and a medical doctor had to get to a village quickly because someone was very ill there. The quickest way was to swim across a river known to be crocodile-infested. The other route would have taken a day. He said that the doctor showed incredible courage in crossing that river, because his imagination was terribly sensitive and he was nearly paralysed with fear throughout the crossing. My friend said that was true courage.

With Saturn in Aries, there is an imbalance in the drive and the reckless courage that goes forward. So these people are often incredibly brave, unbelievably brave. Then they are stopped dead in their tracks by something that stops nobody. It's nothing. Who's afraid of that, except this person? Yet the things that they overcome are enormous, and they don't even know that it is courage. It is an imbalance in courage and recklessness. It is an intensity of desire, an intensity of driving desire, which in this lifetime will be modified and civilised. If nothing else, Saturn is the civilising planet.

Audience: How do you cure a wounded imagination?

Darby: I am not sure that we can cure anything that is connected with Chrion. However, when there is a wound, one has to try to heal it – that is natural. Remember, Chiron is the healer and teacher of heroes. It takes courage to go on a healing journey. If Chiron in fire is a wounded imagination, then it is probably wise to recognise that the wound lies in the way you deal with the gap between your imagination, your vision of reality, and your actions. In Aries, that means you pay attention to what happens between the image that rises out of your natural restlessness to move and change, and the action you take. Your healing journey would consist of small, brave acts. I am thinking of Nelson Mandela here.

Aries rising

This is the most instinctive rising sign in that it simply acts - action is its vehicle - and it has very little awareness of why people react to its actions in the way they do. Look to Mars to see what moves it to act. My friend with Aries rising and Mars in Libra in the 7th house is on the move all the time, either with someone or on her way to someone. I once saw her flare up when a saleswoman would not give me a garment for the sale price, because although it had been on the sales rack, it had been put there inadvertently and it was not really on sale. I said, "It's all right." My friend said, "No, it isn't – it's not fair." And she went off like a firecracker until the manager had to come over and apologise to us. You know, I can't remember if he let me have it for the sale price or not. I just remember the commotion – the buzz of it!

That is something about Aries rising. There is often a commotion. There is excitement and risk, and all in the name of whatever sign Mars is tenanting. People with this Ascendant really do get things happening. But they have to struggle to remember to look for why, when they have trouble with other people. Some of the problem is because the action they take, which is obvious to them, is harmful or insensitive to others.

Outer planets in Aries

Do you realise that we have not had an outer planet in Aries in about sixty years, and we won't for another sixteen years? The **Uranus in Aries** group is a fiery lot. Willful and eccentric and exciting by nature, most of them have it square Pluto in Cancer, and a lot of them, born around 1930, have it square Saturn in Capricorn too. Hard times and hard people – at least the ones who are alive today. This is a tough, demanding group of people who are still fighting the wrongs they see around them. They absolutely hate being boxed in, and if they agree with you about anything for too long, be suspicious. Of course, Uranus in Aries shows up most when it is conjunct personal planets. I know several of them with it conjunct Jupiter in Aries – their notions are very "out there". No reason, no practical argument can daunt their "knowing". They see it, and if you don't, well, you obviously are missing something important!

LEO

We'll discuss the fire of Leo now. In Leo, the fire that burns at one's core, and the images that rise from that fire, express themselves through the planets inhabiting the sign. Any planet in Leo is activated by the feeling of heat that arises from expressing its light in such a way that others receive it with appreciation or love. Planets in Leo are always looking for a Sun in which they might bask, or a bit of shade to rest in before prowling back into the light.

Planets in Leo

Leo is ruled by the Sun, and so it is natural for **the Sun in Leo** to seek and find a place where they can be central and around whom others live their lives, taking warmth from the Leo. Leo Suns need to shine, and they will draw others to them by their warmth or by their capacity to generate an atmosphere where exciting things happen. Not every Leo Sun is warm and generous. The position and aspects to the Moon and Venus and Mars will tell you more about their personal expression, and what happens between themselves and other people. But each Leo Sun carries an image in its heart which puts it at the centre of the stage, and so every Leo generates a field which constellates this stage. Whether it is a happy or unhappy stage depends on other things. I think it must be difficult to be a Leo Sun in this Aquarian climate, where it is not considered politically correct to have the proud and demanding spirit that Leos often exhibit.

Audience: What about Leos whose Sun is conjunct Pluto?

Darby: For the generation with Pluto in Leo, there is the added pressure of every simple act being examined for its darker implications. Their generosity is often suspect and their "ego needs" are considered outdated. Pluto was in Leo from about 1938 to 1958, and so there are a lot of Leo Suns around whose simple need to be the vital centre around which others move and breathe is considered suspect, even by themselves. The Leo principle is being cooked in Pluto's caldron during our time. The natural impulse of these Leos comes up against the evolutionary pressure which demands they undergo some sort of transformational process which will bring them into awareness of the needs of larger and more remote groups of people. But the basic nature of the Sun is to shine. In other signs it will shine through doing that which the sign demands. In Leo it simply shines! It may be overheated by Uranus in Leo, or it may be darkened by Pluto in Leo. Aspects from other planets will tell you what gives it power and what interferes with it, but the image at the heart's core is simple: shine and be glad. Shine and be seen.

Audience: Leos have been having a hard time all around, for a while. Neptune in Scorpio also challenges all the Leos born in that group. And what does Pluto in Scorpio do to the Leos in that group?

Darby: You're right. This is because Pluto is moving so fast these years. But aspects and transits notwithstanding, the Leo Sun will shine – that is its inner mandate and it will do that through whichever house and through whatever aspects it has. It will rarely lose its expectation of love and respect for any length of time, no matter how the times challenge its right to have this expectation.

Audience: Doesn't **Mars in Leo** have that same expectation? "You will love me when I act," or "You will love the action I take!"

Darby: When Mars is in Leo, you must look to the Sun to see what sort of images are lighting the way of this Mars. Mars is always related to the Sun through being its warrior, but when it is in Leo it is even more fiercely connected to its lord. It drives towards creative self-expression. It is lit up by the vision of something "I" can create. And you are probably right – its expectation is to be loved when it goes into action, but also loved for what shines through from the Sun. For example, an Aries with Mars in Leo will be lit up and expect to be appreciated for their courage and innovation.

Audience: And a Gemini Sun for their wit and intelligence?

Darby: Hmmm – and for their sharp retorts when people get too personal, perhaps!

Audience: I have several friends with Mars conjunct Saturn and Pluto.

Darby: A lot of people have that, as Mars was conjunct Saturn and Pluto for a few weeks at the end of 1947, and then again for about six weeks in early 1948. Let me say a bit more about Pluto in Leo, and then I'll say something about Saturn in Leo, and then I'll come back to this.

Pluto in Leo describes a time when a sense of personal identity, qualities of leadership, and creative self-expression – all the things included in Leo's domain – were in the caldron. It occurs in a group of people who are compelled to change the way they naturally express certain things – Leo's things. I don't remember where this comes from, but whoever said it, I like it: Pluto describes the evolutionary task of a generation. Pluto in

Leo destroys and recreates our sense of identity – who we are as a species on this planet.

During the Pluto in Leo time there was a two-and-a-half-year period when Saturn was in Leo, too. Those born with **Saturn in Leo** are having their personal creative expression hammered into shape by the limitations imposed on them through the house Saturn tenants. That's one way of saying it. Saturn in Leo says that the urge to shine is hampered by the need to do it properly, appropriately, usefully, and perfectly. Put Saturn and Pluto together in Leo and you get a group of people who are having their natural urge to shine worked into a useful shape in the volcanic zone where the dark nature of fire is being uncovered. In this case, one parallel might be that we discovered the huge power of fire in the atom bomb.

Audience: Was this useful?

Darby: It was thought to be by those who used it. Saturn conjunct Pluto in Leo has its ego needs worked under great pressure. Pluto says change or die, and Saturn works steadily to shape the light for use. Add Mars and you have all the levels together – personal, impersonal and transpersonal. The desire-driven urge to create, to shine in action, operates within the field where this light is being worked towards usefulness, and there is an intensity about it because there is a sense that if I transform myself, I transform the world.

When this conjunction squares the Sun in Scorpio, then the pressure to create, be useful and transform oneself and the world is great, but it feels right. They may be uncomfortable but they are doing their thing. Taureans often feel more alienated from the frustrations they experience, but as long as they have places of rest and pleasure, they push on with it. Aquarians get caught in fighting it "out there" quite often. And the Leos who have their Sun within that conjunction live the process in their everyday struggle to become fulfilled personally, socially and collectively through their acts of love and creativity.

Audience: But what if...

Darby: Hang on. Let's stop here for lunch. Have you noticed how, every time we go near Pluto territory, it begins to get obsessive?

* * * * *

Are you ready to look at **Jupiter in Leo**? This is a whole different country from where we were before lunch. Does anyone have something to say about this Jupiter?

Audience: Jupiter in Leo gives people a noble image of themselves.

Darby: Yes, they are at best noble, and at worst vainglorious and full of false pride. The image that pulls them towards adventure and the promise of meaning and joy is large and generous and grand. If a Jupiter in Leo person works in a factory which makes doorknobs, they dream of traveling to Rio one day, and seeing "their" doorknobs on doors everywhere, and people being delighted to meet the maker of such lovely and international objects. Jupiter in Leo sees itself as good-hearted and loyal and generous, when it is identifying with its best image of itself. When it identifies too strongly with that image, it is brought down by its darker, petty, smaller side. And when it is in the 7th, it usually sees other people in their own best light.

I am thinking of Marsilio Ficino, with his Jupiter in Leo in the 7th, conjunct Neptune – though he was not aware of that. He saw the bright shining light in those he loved and admired – he probably saw their own best version of themselves. Being a Scorpio with the Sun in the 9th house, that Jupiter gave him the confidence to be a teacher to those he admired so much, even though he had the insecurity of Saturn on the Ascendant in Aquarius, square to his Sun. Always look to the Sun to see whom this Jupiter in Leo is believing in. Ficino's Jupiter in Leo told him he was the teacher to great men, to heroes. And remember, Jupiter carries visions that draw one forward. It does not say what one always is, but what one can be, at one's best.

Audience: What about **Uranus in Leo**?

Darby: Uranus in Leo flashes out images of personal freedom to its group. Those who have personal planets conjunct Uranus in Leo are inspired by some pretty far-out images of what it is possible to be. It is probably saying that, by following your heart, you will find your group, but this group has to experiment with what following its heart means. Experiments succeed and fail. This group has to experiment with creative expression, and whether they are comfortable with this depends on other things, such as how conservative the rest of the chart is.

Look to the Sun, to see what the personal informing image is, and then look to Uranus in Leo to see where this personal working out of destiny will become radical. I have a Uranus in Leo friend with Sun conjunct Mercury in Capricorn in the 4th, and lots of planets in the 3rd. He has Moon in Leo, in the 10th, but it is not conjoined to Uranus, which is in the 11th. He is a novelist, and he encounters all kinds of groups in all sorts of ways, and these various groups arise in his books in unexpected ways. The books shock, delight, enrage, enlighten, and turn people's visions of themselves upside down. He sees himself as simply doing his work. But he does notice the powerful reactions people have.

Now, let me say something about the personal planets, Moon and Mercury and Venus in Leo. Remember, always refer to the Sun and its central direction, because it tells you where these planets are getting their image from. If the Sun is in Leo and Mercury is too, then the information-gathering service gets its information from the same place as the Sun gets its message to shine. But when the Sun is in Virgo or Cancer, one receives information through images that go straight to one's heart, and that can be awkward for the Sun. One relates to information very personally and communicates passionately with Mercury in Leo, and that heats up the Virgo and doesn't make it the cool customer it imagines itself to be. It also heats up Cancerian waters, and sometimes brings the Cancerian into a brighter light than they mean to be in. Whatever the Cancerian feels most protective about is translated into passionate language by the images Mercury snapshots.

Venus in Leo usually sees the mother as the centre of attention when the person is young, and this is either a happy or unhappy image to carry. There is often ambivalence about being the centre of attention oneself. The Sun will tell what is most valued by the Venus in Leo person, and they will love best those who appreciate their gifts. One must be appreciated for one's best light – when this doesn't happen, the fire dims and the sense of personal value fades. Creative self-expression is always the path back to the light, when Venus in Leo is feeling lonely or unloved. The image in the fire demands that one be creative, and it offers happy rewards for the effort.

I am thinking of a Cancerian man whose creative gifts of love come through his cooking. He has built the kitchen so the stove is in the middle of the room, and he cooks while everyone sits around him! His Moon is in the 6th, and so he is also satisfying his need to nurture his huge family through this service. But the way he does it is pure Venus in Leo.

Audience: You once said that those with **Moon in Leo** have queens for mothers, and whether they are good queens or bad, the Leo Moon is loyal to them. Can you say something about that?

Darby: The Sun will tell how the Leo Moon deals with its mother. A Capricorn will judge her and demand she be a creative person in her own right. But they will also demand a great deal from her in the relationship, as the demands of the Capricorn Sun are very powerful, and this Moon receives its images straight from the heat of the Sun. A Gemini Sun will try to communicate with her and understand her. They will suffer greatly if they are not central to her. Their communication skills develop rapidly, once they find people who light up when they are talking.

Audience: I'm a Cancerian with Leo Moon. It seems backwards to me.

Darby: Do you bully your mother into her best behaviour?

Audience: Well, she wouldn't do anything if I didn't!

Darby: Aha. The key to the Leo Moon, again, rests in the Sun. The images that inform the Leo Moon demand that life be a creative process, and they suffer if their lives are hampered by too many mundane concerns. Day-to-day life will be a drama in one way or another – whether happy or unhappy depends on other things.

Planets in the 5th house

Audience: How does this all relate to the 5th house?

Darby: Planets in Leo move from a central fire that puts them centre stage. Planets in Leo are always taking their image from the spirit of the natal Sun, and probably some of their action can be seen as moving from the progressed Sun. I have not thought about that enough lately to develop it here. Planets in the 5th house – unless they are in Leo – are sort of surprised into the limelight when they are in 5th house territory.

Audience: What?

Darby: Okay, let's play with this a bit. The 5th house is the house of love affairs, creativity and children. I call it the house of "the children of the body and the mind". I picked that up from some-one years ago, but I have said it this way for so long that it feels like mine.

Audience: 'Mediocre minds imitate, great minds steal', eh?

Darby: Oh! We are definitely in the 5th house now! Party time! Well, that's what happens when planets are in the 5th house – they seem to heat up in the light. Do you want to know what kind of a party person you are? Look at your 5th house. Do you want to know how you get into love affairs? Look to your 5th house and, of course, the ruler of the cusp. I have two friends who have been married for thirty-five years. She has Saturn in Aquarius in the 5th, and he has Uranus in Pisces in the 5th trine his Sun-Jupiter in the 9th. He plays the piano, he sings, he dances, he laughs and weeps with others when they have a party. She cooks the food perfectly, and sits primly in the corner having serious conversa-tions. I once asked her if she found it difficult that they were so different. She said, "Oh no, it's fine," but I wondered if perhaps it had not always been fine – there must have been some difficulty in the early days.

They have two children who both consider her a very fine person, but fairly rigid and narrow intellectually. They both know their father loves them very much, but he has always been somewhat distant. They think of him as very wise. They remember her as strict. And so on. They each have their separate relationships with their parents, but their general memories of their parents in childhood refer to their parents' 5th house. Look at your parents' 5th house and see if you can connect to what I am saying. How did your mother or father play with you? Look at your own 5th house – how do you play with your children? How do you play? Capricorn on the cusp of the 5th will enjoy very different plays, movies, and parties than Sagittarius on the 5th, and if they are both in the 5th, then you will find the combination in whatever area the creative life touches.

Audience: Does the 5th say something about your relationship with children in general?

Darby: Yes, I think it does. Your Moon will always be active when you are around children, but the 5th house cusp and planets in the 5th will tell you how you "play" with them. Also, it will tell you where you are competing with the children in your life! And that will tell you where you are uncomfortable with children.

Audience: And where you are uncomfortable with the child part of yourself?

Darby: Yes, and again, we always have to look at the Moon when we are in any territory that refers us back to childhood conditioning. But the 5th house and the position and condition of its ruler will tell you how you enter the space where creative self-expression has the stage.

Audience: I have Aquarius on the cusp of the 5th, and Uranus in the 9th, and Saturn in the 11th in Virgo. I have always thought of myself as pretty free and liberal when it comes to my children. They grew up with some fairly unconventional notions, astrology being a normal conversation at home. But if I think of Saturn partaking of the rulership, I notice that I am very sensitive to what my friends think about my children. My son came back from backpacking in South America last year and decided to join his father's bank. I was shocked. I can't decide whether I am proud of him or embarrassed by him! I am a painter, and I am now noticing that I feel the same way about my paintings – I let them flow out of me as they will, and then I am very sensitive if I feel anyone is judging them. I guess this is where I take myself more seriously than I thought.

Darby: And you have Leo on the eleventh house cusp?

Audience: Yes, and I definitely shine best in groups. In fact, I lead groups and am confident doing that. I have the Saturnian need to know what my role is in a group – and I am happy when I know my role and can shine there.

Darby: You have given us some very good connections here. Thank you. The house ruled by Leo will be the house where your Sun will go to shine. That's odd, because, of course, the house where your Sun lives will be the area of life which is lit up by the Sun, and you will be drawn there to act out your destiny. But if you notice, the house which Leo cusps will draw the Sun there as someone beloved, but away, draws your heart's thoughts. Whatever planets are in that house will be a factor in what happens when you are drawn to shine there. Saturn in that house will say, "You may shine here, but only if you have carefully set the circumstances and you take responsibility for your role." Jupiter or Venus there will call you with a joyous heart. Mars in Leo in the house which Leo cusps will draw you there because it is there that the most exciting challenges lie for you.

Leo rising

Leo rising people appear to be completely at ease with who they are. They sit and walk and move in such a way that you feel they know who they are and they are confident with it. Whether this is true behind the scenes depends on other things. But when they enter rooms with people in them, they do so with grace and ease. No matter what is happening beneath the surface, they "put on a show" for the punters! Life is dramatic because everything is filtered through the fire of the Sun.

This is the place where the Sun comes to shine, though it will normally live somewhere else, in another house. The Sun, its natal house and aspects, tell you who is there behind the role of this rising sign – but whatever the Sun, it lives itself out in a personally dramatic way. Leo rising does not like to be overlooked or ignored, unless it has decided that this is the role it is playing today – and then it doesn't like to be noticed. It all depends on what is being played out on this or another day. Remember, it is the Sun which is shining on this person as they enter the stage of life, and so you must look to the natal Sun to see what image is back-lighting this Leo rising. This rising sign is being directed by the Sun – no wonder it appears so confident!

SAGITTARIUS

This is the sign that takes us into the most subtle realms of fire. Sagittarian fire lights up the world in such a way that large patterns are seen at once. Planets in Sagittarius move from images which offer satisfying possibilities if they are followed. This is the sign that takes us to the boundaries of our known world, and then lures us into adventures that will take us beyond. The images usually promise huge rewards. Those with planets in this sign imagine that, by going beyond that which is familiar, they will arrive at a place where everything will be understood, and the understanding will be joyous. Other planets in other signs may limit the reach of planets in Sagittarius, but the images continue to arise, calling them to adventure.

Not everyone with planets in this sign travels the world, nor do they all have access to higher education. Sometimes the adventures are purely in the realm of imagination. I have noticed that the more planets in Sagittarius, the more likely the experiences are imaginal. This is a restless fire. The images that lure keep changing. People with planets in Sagittarius are often accused of being lazy – they seem to have so much potential, but they need time to dream in their fiery way. They need to wander around while the images play through the layers of their minds and hearts. When they get going, they move with clarity and directness, but there are so many possibilities. Images rise but disappear quickly, and they have to wait for the one that will shoot them forward, making the potential actual.

I'd like to say something about the 9th house right now, because I am going to show you two charts before tea, and we may want to fill in all sorts of gaps in the last session. The two charts are heavily Sagittarian, and so we will explore the Sagittarian domain while we are discussing them.

Planets in the 9th house

What about planets in the 9th house? What happens to them?

Audience: They get educated.

Darby: Brilliant! They do get educated. Any planet in the 9th, from the Sun to Saturn, is sent on a trip from fairly early in life. Those with the Sun there often have fathers who were away a lot of the time, and so they imagine their fathers out there somewhere, rather than here now. Those with Mars in the 9th often come into contact with other religions or cultures very early, and this makes them somewhat rebellious spiritually, later on. Mercury there hears or reads stories of other lands early, and is restless until it can move!

No matter how earthed planets in the 9th house are, by sign or aspect, they are dragged out of themselves to the borders of their known world from the moment they begin to know there are any borders at all. It is the house of higher education, long-distance travel, the higher law courts – all sorts of things that are beyond ordinary reach. Even today we have to re-educate ourselves about the 9th house, because long-distance travel changes every time they make a faster plane, bus or train. Some of us, many of you here today, go back and forth to the Continent so easily and frequently that it has to be classed as short-distance travel. But there are still people all over the planet for whom ten miles is long-distance travel. Remember this when you are doing charts. The 9th house is a house where you must adjust your perspective each time you enter it.

Audience: What is the difference between Venus in Sagittarius and Venus in the 9th?

Darby: When I think of Venus in Sagittarius, I think of its wild romanticism, its idealism, its inner flame lit up by exotic, imaginative or even dangerous relationships. Venus in the 9th, in earth or air or water, may be taken on a wild and romantic journey by love, but it is not necessarily wild or exotic itself. Venus in Sagittarius leaps into the whitewater rapids of love without a packet of tea or a first aid kit. Venus in the 9th, in other elements, gets into the canoe, but it takes its own luggage with it. Remember, Venus in Sagittarius is informed by a Jupiterian image. Venus in the 9th is informed by the reality of its ruler. Venus in Capricorn in the 9th has Saturn as its lord, and though it may travel, and love those from foreign parts, and love education, it is still Saturnian and therefore somewhat conservative in its principles. Venus in the 9th gets educated by love. Venus in Sagittarius is an education in love.

Let's take a look at Saturn in the 9th house. In this case Saturn is taken on a journey, via education or travel of one kind or another, so it can get educated. Through whatever journeys it goes on, the person with this position will develop certain aspects of character which will bring some sort of authority. Saturn will be informed by whatever planet rules the sign it is in. I have a friend with Saturn in the 9th in Virgo, so hers is ruled by Mercury. Mercury is in Aries and rules the 5th house, and she has done pioneering work in her field, writing books, lecturing and making films. Now in her forties, she is invited to universities all over the world to teach her techniques, which have to do with pain management in sick children. She has earned an authoritative position through long and careful observation and the development of imaginative techniques. She has worked very hard to achieve this position because she believes in her work. She has Sagittarius rising with Sun conjunct Jupiter in Pisces, so as you can imagine, she has always believed in her destiny to help and heal very strongly. But with Saturn in the 9th, she has had to work a long time to earn the recognition she deserved. Wherever Saturn is, long hard work brings reward. It's such a cliché, but it is so true.

Uranus, Neptune or Pluto in the 9th seem to bring strange experiences. People with these positions are connected to some kind of collective or transpersonal or spiritual transmitters in some way. How they interpret what they get through their imaginations, and what they do with the interpretation, has to do with other factors in the chart and in themselves. I had a very close friend who was a Sagittarian. She had Jupiter conjunct Neptune in Cancer in the 9th, opposite Uranus in the 3rd in Capricorn. She was an artist in all sorts of media, and extraordinarily connected to something beyond her ability to interpret. She tried and tried to find something that would make sense of her visions. She read voraciously. She had Moon in Libra in the 12th, and Libra rising, but no other air. Even her art could not quite express what she intuited. It was very frustrating for her, but she kept trying all the way to her end. In her eighties, her art became so luminous that even she felt that it was beginning to express what she knew.

Sagittarius rising

Audience: I have two sons with Sagittarius rising, and they are both clowns. My brother has it too, and when he comes to visit, our house becomes like a circus.

Darby: If a client is coming with Sagittarius rising, I assume he or she will be open, friendly, and have a great sense of humour. This is generally true. I think that the key to this rising sign is that it imagines itself to be on foreign tour here. It is often amazed and amused at the habits of the "natives". Many of them treat themselves as local inhabitants too, telling stories against themselves that make other people laugh and shake their heads at the folly of humankind. Jupiter in the chart points to where it gets lit up and interested, because it has an idea that this is where the truth will be found. In those moments when it thinks it has the truth, it will tell you! It is generally considered a "lucky" rising sign. That is because it is often filled with enthusiasm for things – it approaches life with dreams of future possibility leading it on. Do you recognise that?

Audience: Yes, but there is a strange thing happening. I have always thought of myself as free, footloose, on my way to another trek as soon as I get the chance. But now that I'm in my forties, I notice that I have been married for eighteen years and have a house and a mortgage and kids, and I'm a bit confused about whether I am the adventurer I thought I was. Pluto is on my Ascendant at the moment.

Darby: So you may lose your vision for a time, while it gets brought up to date. I have noticed that about Sagittarius rising – it has a vision of itself which is very strong, and which is always taking it into future possibilities. When it gets dampened for a time, it must be very disconcerting – as if a light goes out on the pathway ahead.

Audience: But the rising sign is an unconscious part of us, isn't it?

Darby: We don't consciously identify with it unless there are other planets close to it, and then we may identify with that planet's nature in the sign. But we do become identified with the planet that rules the rising sign. Sagittarius rising will be known by his or her Jupiter, but may not be conscious of the fact that he or she is always living in the light of some future possibility of freedom and knowledge. It forgets that it is a future possibility that is lighting its way, and it imagines itself in that possibility now. Then something happens to dim the light for a time, and it gets a bit confusing. But in time the way lights up again. Enthusiasm and optimism go together, don't they?

And to return to your original question, a Sagittarius Sun *knows* it lives by a vision, a principle, a philosophy – it *knows* it has a guiding star. From the awakening of its consciousness, it is there. It can point to it, discuss it, and argue about it. Its way is lit by this light. Jupiter will describe where it gets this from, or what feeds it.

Rather than talk about Sagittarius any more, what I would like to do is to show you two charts where planets in Sagittarius are very powerful. In fact, the fire signs are dominant in these two charts. By looking at them, we will not only get some understanding of Sagittarian fire, but also of fire in general.

TWO FIRE CHARTS

I would like you to look at these two charts for a few minutes without thinking about who they might be.

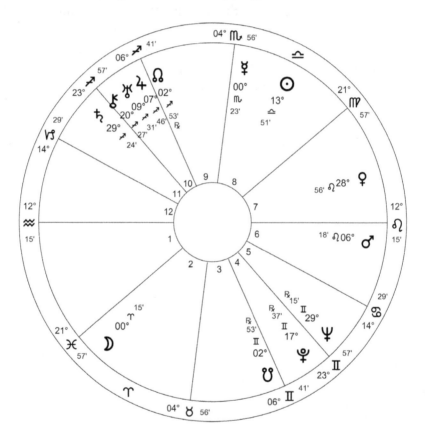

Chart 1
7 October 1900, 3.30 pm, München
Koch cusps

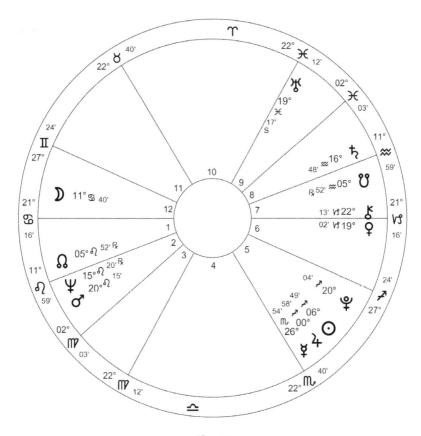

Chart 2
28 November 1757, 7.00 pm, London
Koch cusps

Both of these are the charts of men, and both are very fiery. Both of them were very clear about their beliefs, and both translated their vision into action, and so both had an effect on their world. Yet one translated that vision in such a way that he is known to us as a truly evil man. When we hear his name, we sense something about the power of Darkness. The other man expressed his vision in such a way that we remember him as a good man, a man who loved the Light, a visionary who fought the right things and fostered the right ideals.

Audience: They both have Jupiter in Sagittarius. One has it conjunct his Sun, and the other has it conjunct Uranus. I would imagine that the first chart had the greater effect on the world, because of that Jupiter conjunct Uranus at the MC. Both have Mars in Leo square Mercury in Scorpio. So both are impatient and see themselves at the centre of the action, with insights others don't have.

Audience: The first might be some kind of religious leader with that Jupiter at the MC, but it would be strange in some way, with the conjunction to Uranus. The second chart has Uranus in Pisces in the 9th house, and so I imagine he saw faeries at the bottom of the garden, and is fairly eccentric in his views.

Audience: The first chart has the Moon in a T-square, out of sign, but very tight: Moon square Saturn in Sagittarius opposite Neptune in Gemini. It must be uncomfortable to have such a strong Jupiter, and then Saturn in Sagittarius. Was he judged by the collective for his strange beliefs? I am looking at his Saturn in the 11th house.

Audience: I have just noticed that both have Saturn opposite Neptune, and as I have that, I wonder if they were both a bit paranoid? If I get too caught up in Saturn's reality, I start getting heavy and judgmental. I lose touch with my feelings and get into all sorts of emotional trouble. And if I get too Neptunian I forget to pay my rent and my landlord comes down heavily on me – so I'm always a bit edgy.

Darby: Very interesting, all of your insights. All right, the first is the chart of Heinrich Himmler. The second chart is William Blake.

Heinrich Himmler

Let's look more closely at Himmler's chart first. He was the chief of the SS in Hitler's army. He saw himself as a teacher and reformer who was born to change the world: Sagittarius on the MC and Jupiter conjunct Uranus right there, in the 10th house. The conjunction is trine his 6th house Mars in Leo – the image in the fire of his Mars showed himself as this teacher and reformer. Mars in Leo refers back to his Sun, ruler of Leo, and that Sun is in the 8th in Libra, sextile the conjunction in the 10th and sextile Mars. "I am the reformer – the transformer." Well, yes, he was. He designed the concentration camps where millions of people died.

Himmler was connected to the fiery realm where unfolding and infinite potential swirls in the fires of creation, and those with fiery planets see glimpses of those images. Eve Jackson quotes Stephen Arroyo in her book on Jupiter: "People with Uranus conjunct Jupiter have weird ideas." Through his Jupiter-Uranus conjunction he "saw" the new and better world that his work would give birth to. With the conjunction in Sagittarius, his ideas were over-the-top weird.

He was a visionary, but there was something deeply missing there. He is constantly referred to as a "nonentity" and as having a "colourless personality". He seemed completely insignificant, though he rose to unimaginable power. He was, nearly to the end, devoted to Hitler, and he must have been devoted to others, too, on his way to Hitler, with his Venus in Leo in the 7th. He would have seen himself achieving power "on the stage" of life through those he worshipped. His Venus in Leo carried an image which would put him centre stage, through his (7th house) "other". As Leo then refers back to the Sun in the 8th in Libra, we might wonder what it is he saw himself as balancing. As the balancer, the mutual reception between the Sun and Venus would have made him choose powerful people who would give him the

power to bring the world he imagined into balance – to transform it into a beautiful world!

*"We must be honest, decent, loyal, and comradely to members
of our own blood, and to nobody else. What happens to a
Russian, to a Czech, does not interest me in the slightest."*
– Heinrich Himmler

His Moon in Aries is trine the Jupiter-Uranus conjunction
and square to Neptune on one side and Saturn on the other.
I imagine he enjoyed being generous – it vitalised him and,
with Aquarius rising, he was an odd mixture of qualities coming out in unpredictable ways. He came across as insignificant
and rather mediocre, until he was in a private group where he

could express his ideas, and then he was enthusiastic and vivacious. When he was finally given a castle, he had parties where everyone would dress up. He was kind to children and animals. He was sentimental and emotional, as most of that lot were. He imagined himself as kind and generous and religious. However, he could not imagine himself as a Jew – they became a vision of something that had to be burned out of the body of humanity so that it could fulfill its "glorious purpose".

Audience: I'm looking at that Saturn in the 11th house, which might show where the shadow of all that bright Sagittarius vision lives. He dumped all the light's shadow on groups other than his own. And the opposition from Saturn and Chiron to Neptune – strange ideas, in other words, ideas that were not the ones he identified with, made him paranoid.

Darby: Yes, his Saturn in Sagittarius in the 11th house could only imagine those who could share his vision of the "better world" – he felt uncomfortable with people and with groups whose religion or philosophy was different to his. He was very religious – can you imagine? He wanted to be Minister of Religious Affairs, and wouldn't let anyone into his cabinet unless they were church-going men and professed belief in God!

Audience: Look at that opposition squaring his Aries Moon. I wonder if he was personally hurt by those who belonged to other groups when he was young. Or perhaps his mother was, and he picked up the paranoia from her. The Moon is also quincunx Mercury in Scorpio in the 8th, which is square Mars in Leo, which is trine the Moon.

Darby: Yes, he was attuned to receiving information which hurt his pride (the square to Mars), which was not properly absorbed by his feelings (quincunx the Moon in Aries) and which galvanised him into action (trine the Mars in the 6th). He was often ill with headaches and intestinal complaints, and he became hysterical with fear and pain each time he had an attack. You can imagine how wild his fantasies got when he was "attacked" in his body. Those aspects show a kind of fiery roller-coaster. It all circles around beautifully. The archetypal realm of images was accessible to him through his fire, and his personal nature picked it up and translated it according to his distortions. It was too much for his body and his psyche to bear. He picked up the distortions and the pure vision with his mother's milk – the Moon is in the 2nd.

Audience: Do you know that he had his own astrologer and went to him for advice? And yet he also persecuted astrologers because he knew how dangerous they could be with their ability to predict the future. His own astrologer went to Buchenwald for a while, and when he was released, Himmler said to him, "Did anyone treat you badly? Give me their names and I will have them shot in the morning." Mr. Nice Guy.

Audience: That was part of the massive contradiction. The one thing that the Nazis really hated about astrology was that it wouldn't support their theory of the Aryan master race, and yet they tried to get astrologers to predict that the master race would win and conquer the rest of the world.

Audience: What's interesting about Himmler is that he set up the symbols and the SS all according to astrological moments, and yet he feared astrologers and persecuted them. I once read that he knew about the plot against Hitler, did nothing, but went to an astrologer. It is on record that he asked the astrologer if Hitler would survive the attempt on his life. He probably imagined himself taking over once Hitler was out of the way.

Darby: Well, although the scale of his madness was greater than most, his attempt to get the answers he wanted from astrologers seems pretty normal. A lot of people come to us wanting us to fix the future for them so they will get what they want.

However, his "love" for astrology was part of his obsession with the occult. Having a window, however distorted, onto the wider universe of infinite potential, he knew that there was truth and reality in things that ordinary people couldn't imagine. He was obsessed with finding the spear that pierced Christ's side, the "Spear of Destiny", because he was certain that it would be the means of conquering the world. His Moon in the 2nd wanted a physical object that would release the vision.

Audience: Chiron is in Sagittarius – and it is in opposition to Pluto. In his case, his "wounded imagination" drove towards destruction, rather than healing.

Darby: Yes, but he thought he was healing the world by what he was destroying! Many people born around that time would have had that opposition. However, with all his fire, his participation in the collective "wounded imagination" which felt under threat from alien ideas – Pluto in Gemini – certainly added a hot and dangerous wind to the already wild contact with realms which give us a sense of future potential.

We don't know what makes someone good or evil. When the war was lost, he killed his wife, his children and his dog. These might have been acts of kindness from his point of view, and he may have been right. Once the allies arrived, he tried to escape, was caught, and killed himself immediately. He apparently never understood why people didn't love him. Can you imagine who lived in there? Was there anyone home at all? There does not seem to be any controlling factor – no ego-self who could choose what to believe of all the images firing his imagination.

Think of the fancies that take over your imagination at times. You are walking down a street and you imagine danger, but there is none. You fancy someone is being unkind to you, and later you find out they had a headache when you phoned them about something or other. You imagine you have finally "arrived" and now your life will go smoothly because of this or that inner or outer circumstance. Well, this man had all his fire joined up, so to speak, and it simply ran through him without check. It fell foul of his emotional particularities, represented by that Moon and its aspects, but there seems to have been no one home to do a reality test, especially as reality seemed to be colluding with him for quite a stretch of time, allowing him to believe his own stories.

Audience: I keep being drawn to that Venus in Leo in the 7th. It is part of a yod, sextile Mercury in Scorpio and both quincunx the Moon, which is in that T-square. It must indicate some sort of passionate longing to be understood and loved, but an emotional nature that cannot connect to others.

Audience: One thing I read was that, at the Nuremberg trials, the Nazis would never accept that they were wrong. They just said, "You don't understand that what we were trying to do had to be done." Curiously, the ones that were hung were then burnt in Dachau. What a circle that is – to be burnt in your own fire.

Darby: Charles [Harvey] has said that most of the Nazi gang had very strong Jupiters. Interesting conclusion to a Jupiterian life! In Himmler's case, with the conjunction to Uranus trine the Moon and Mars, it is quite a whirling wheel of fire. If you add the Saturn-Neptune opposition square the Moon, you get quite a powerful mixing of signals. His Moon in Aries trine Mars in Leo imagined himself as a warrior – trine the Jupiter-Uranus conjunction – who would enlighten and free the world. Now he is remembered as a madman who was part of a mad gang of thugs, which fortunately self-destructed in the end, but not before doing immense harm all around.

We could see this chart as the chart of someone used by something beyond our recognised chain of causality. But we have to assume he had a modicum of free will, and that at some point he chose to go with it. He has no earth, and so we might say he was not inhibited by anything we might call "common sense". He has one water planet – Mercury in Scorpio in the 8th – and it is quincunx his intensely configured Moon. This is a lot of pressure from the hidden realm of feelings, and it hasn't got any safe channel, so to speak.

He became possessed by something that was burning in the collective imagination at the time. He became a forcefield. Sometimes earthquakes wipe out entire civilisations. So do volcanoes. You know the one that erupted in 1500 BCE on the Greek island of Santorini? You can still feel the power of what happened there. Himmler and his gang of hoodlums were some sort of volcano. In his case there was no ground on which to stand, and no feelings that connected him enough to other human beings. He became a forcefield, he became a bush fire, he became a volcano, and he was responsible for as many people dying as lava has been in our long history.

Audience: Lava is liquid fire.

Darby: It is. There is really nothing there to control all that fire, unless we see the Saturn opposition Pluto as the invisible or, you might say, divine retribution which stopped him, ultimately. And even then, he took his own life – no one else did it to him. What makes a man receptive to the visionary realms in such a way that he becomes a force for evil? We have always wondered about this, and different ages and different cultures come up with different ideas. But we really don't know.

Let's look at the other fiery chart now.

William Blake

William Blake was born on the 28th of November, 1757, in London. I have used the 7:00 p.m. chart although I have seen one for 7:30 and also one for 7:45. They all have Cancer rising with Moon in the 12th, but some of the planets slip into earlier houses. Blake was one of England's great mystic poets and, of course, artists too. He is a rare mystic in that he was not attached to any particular religion; in fact he was deeply anti-religious.

He who does not imagine in stronger and better lineaments,
and in stronger and better light than his perishing
and mortal eye can see, does not imagine at all.

– William Blake

Audience: What about the Society of Inner Light, Madame Blavatsky, and so on? They are all part of a tradition of unorthodox mysticism.

Darby: You are right. You do have a tradition, at least in the last century or so, of giving space, if not immediate respect, to the secular mystic. William Blake has achieved much more recognition and respect than most of those who have spoken straight from the visionary fire.

At the age of three or four, Blake had his first vision. His parents decided that school would be harmful to him, so they never sent him, and he was educated at home – with the result that his imagination was not tampered with by convention. At about eleven or twelve, his father sent him to engraving college, because he wanted to give him a skill. His father was certainly well intentioned, and chose a training that was useful to his creative life, but William felt oppressed by it. Look at that Mars in Leo conjunct Neptune opposing Saturn – the 2nd to the 8th. He became an engraver, but he felt spiritually enslaved by his engraving work. Others found him so difficult to deal with that he hardly ever made any money. But he said that he chose to live in poverty all his life because the goddess Fortuna was a whore! His Mars in Leo was moved by the image of himself as carrying the light of the spiritual world – Sun conjunct Jupiter in Sagittarius, in the 5th – through his creative work! And with Neptune in Leo's fire, too, he would have been drawn to even more powerful images of himself as the one who could bring through the light of that world.

Audience: You say, "the light of the spiritual world", in referring to his Mars in Leo, but in Himmler's case you didn't use that phrase.

Darby: True, but look to the Sun when you see planets in Leo, as the origin of the image moving the planet. In Himmler's case the Sun is in Libra in the 8th house, in mutual reception to his Venus in the 7th, as we discussed. Blake's Mars in Leo gets its informing image from Sun conjunct Jupiter in Sagittarius, in the 5th. You see? Different "signatures" – different "heart's desires" in each case.

He was married for forty-five years to his Kate, but he probably married her on the rebound. We can imagine that to be true, as he had Venus in Capricorn on the cusp of the 7th conjunct Chiron in Capricorn in the 7th. They are opposition the Moon in Cancer in the 12th house. His first love was with a sort of early feminist. Socially she was "above his station" – and that mattered. That was "the matter" with his Capricorn Venus. Around the time of his marriage he wrote: "I curse my stars in bitter grief and woe / That made my love so high and me so low."

He fell in love first with someone "above him" socially (Venus in Capricorn on the cusp of the 7th), but his true wife (his Moon in "ordinary" Cancer in the 12th) was the illiterate daughter of a market gardener. And she was emotionally behind him all their life, supportive to all he did throughout their materially impoverished and imaginatively rich life. She apparently bored him in the beginning, but they were very happy in the end.

Let me say something here about fire and love. Fire is heat and passion, and therefore fire is expressed very naturally through love. But fire's love is terribly romantic, and Sagittarian fire is especially so. It perceives the innate potential in those that it gets fired up by, and when it later has to deal with all sorts of muddy layers, it gets very shocked. Very fiery people seem to "imagine" you in your potentially perfect state, but then the time-shaped details get in the way. This can be a problem. Look at Blake's chart, with those five planets in fire – his vision was so clear, and he found it enraging that the establishment could not see what he could.

He hated the Church, but he did not hate Christ. He said that Christ was The Imagination. He spent huge amounts of energy in fighting every kind of authority. He fought religion; he fought government. He thought that they were extremely dangerous, and that they enslaved, and that they enchained our minds and our spirits. If he was living today, he would be fighting the medical authorities, government, and the big corporations, I imagine.

Audience: He hated the whole rise of rationalism in the 18th century.

Audience: It was the institutionalisation of religion that he couldn't stand – the way it had become encrusted with laws and regulations. "And Priests in black gowns, were walking their rounds / And binding with briars, my joys and desires."

Darby: Yes, from *Songs of Experience*. I have that here. Let me read it to you:

> I went to the Garden of Love.
> And saw what I never had seen:
> A Chapel was built in the midst,
> Where I used to play on the green.
>
> And the gates of this Chapel were shut,
> And Thou shall not, writ over the door;
> So I turn'd to the Garden of Love,
> That so many sweet flowers bore,
>
> And I saw that it was filled with graves,
> And tomb-stones where flowers should be:
> And Priests in black gowns, were walking their rounds,
> And binding with briars, my joys & desires.

From a psychological point of view, he projected his Saturn in Aquarius in the 8th onto those in power. He then fought them with all his creative power. We might wonder about his picture of his father. We know he resented having been sent to learn engraving, but the cold judgement of Saturn in the 8th goes deeper than that. Saturn here shows that he had a cold and unrelenting streak in his nature, through which he saw his "enemies". He was very fortunate in that he had the vehicle of his art through which to express himself. Otherwise he might have been ground into bitterness by what he saw as the truth, which had been distorted and corrupted by the Church and by the State. Unless one can find an outlet for fire, it turns against oneself. Those who burn with vision must be able to express it so that others receive some of the heat.

He has Moon in Cancer, and so over time the background support of his Kate must have nourished his waters in a way that nourished his very spirit. Do you see how it is in an applying trine to Uranus in the 9th house? Whether you take Jupiter or Neptune as the ruler of the 9th house, both are in fire and both refer to his creative vision and its expression – Neptune in Leo and Jupiter conjunct the Sun in the 5th.

In the end he wrote about love, and he died singing! His last words were to his Kate about the gift of love. He developed through his day-to-day loving, and I think this is because he put his fire into his art. Because he had an outlet for his fire, he was able to navigate by it, rather than being consumed by it. He loved his desire, he loved his passion, but was neither consumed by it nor did he suppress it. If he had had Venus in Sagittarius, too, it may have been harder to work at his personal loving in the way he did. He would have been disillusioned by the "clay" surrounding the spirit of the one he loved. But with his Venus in Capricorn, it seems he could endure, and he brought his fiery vision into his marriage. He wrote a poem some time into the marriage, which I don't think was published in his lifetime.

Seek Love in the Pity of other's Woe,
In the gentle relief of another's care,
In the darkness of night & the winter's snow,
In the naked & outcast, Seek Love there!

The 5th house is the house of "love affairs, creativity and children". I think of it as the house where one sees the sort of love affair one can have with life itself. He has Scorpio on the cusp of the 5th, Mercury in Scorpio there, and then the three planets in Sagittarius. His love affair with life was very intense, but when he was hurt by life he lashed out with his Mercury in Scorpio. He did it through the hard work of engraving his poems and his drawings, for which he received little money but, I'll bet, a lot of emotional satisfaction! Mars in Leo is in the 2nd, opposite Saturn in the 8th. He was considered eccentric, mad, stubborn and visionary. Is this not a good description of the reputation of a man with Uranus on the MC in Pisces? Now we think of him as a genius – he had faith in the future of his art. His voice was prophetic – pure Sagittarius.

He had a few friends who honoured him greatly and believed in him and in his visionary powers. He never sold a painting in his life, like Van Gogh, who was also very fiery; but Blake didn't care, in a truly fiery way. He had his great audience in the sky. He thought his times were filled with people so corrupt and lost that he didn't need to speak to them. He said his heavenly hosts told him that he would be famous, and that his words would be heard in the future. He said, "I labour upwards into futurity." That is one of the secrets of Sagittarian fire. It intuits the shape of the future and it draws inspiration from what it sees. It is working for the potential that it can perceive in the future.

Liz once said that the most interesting thing for fire people is the conversation they have with the genie. His angels, his hosts, his heavenly conversations nourished his soul. This is fire and water working together! He loved the Bible. I think he related more to the Old Testament than the New – at least, this seems obvious if we look at his drawings and read his poems. He spoke to Ezekiel and he spoke to the saints. He had conversations with them in his room. He was in direct contact with that archetypal realm. His fiery Jupiter, Sun and Pluto were all in Sagittarius and in the 5th house. There was nothing to impede his direct access to the imaginal realm.

Audience: Was his work channeled?

Darby: Channeled? We might say that now, but I don't think he would have said it that way. He was simply having conversations with angels. He created a new form of art. There was no precedence for it, and there have been no followers. He was painting and drawing things that only he could see. All mystics "see" into the fiery realms, but not all have poetic gifts and a hard training in etching! All fiery people "see" right into the imaginal plane, but not all have the opportunity, the discipline and the drive to turn what they see into art.

He lived to be sixty-nine years old. He only left London once. He said that London manifested God everywhere. He saw eternity in the London streets, which he said were full of the human awful wonder of God. Remember that, folks, when you are slogging through another gray miserable day! He saw God in the concrete, and he lived in a pretty nasty time of London's history. There were mob riots daily because there was so much poverty and despair. He lived in poverty, but not despair. With his fiery Mars-Neptune in the 2nd opposite Saturn in the 8th, he worked hard not to get money!

He didn't like drawing from nature, because he said it was drawing from dead things! For him it was the imaginal realm which was alive. The "real world" was the imaginal world. He loved nature but really only as it expressed the fire of creation. This man was not your earthy type!

Audience: "To see the world in a grain of sand..."

Audience: If you think of it, all of his paintings look like flames.

Darby: He said, "Natures deadens. It weakens the imagination in me." That's why he stayed in the city. Picasso had only one planet in fire, but it was a Sagittarius Moon in the 5th house – and he had Leo rising. He once said that it was a bit of a waste that he had all that money and could live in wonderful places, because he didn't really need all that external beauty to get inspired. William Blake's inspiration for his art and his whole way of life came from within.

He thought that institutions which society made up were deadening; they killed the imagination, killed the spirit. So he worked through his anger and resentment and frustration about where society was at, to manifest his vision. He had one planet in air. If you have any planets in air and you have fire, it will always go for air first. It will look to express itself through air first, and then it will interact with the other planets.

Audience: He said, "Brothels are built with bricks and religion." He railed against the repression of the expression of sexuality – Sun-Jupiter in the 5th and that Saturn in the 8th. So I guess he had to be trying to liberate sexuality.

Darby: Yes, interesting, isn't it? He was once approached by an Anglican priest, Rev. Dr. Trussler, who wanted his "moral tales" illustrated. Big mistake! Blake illustrated them with cavorting angels, and the Reverend Doctor was completely outraged. He refused them, and went to someone else, and complained to others of Blake, who, he said was "dimmed with superstition". Blake wrote him a long letter expressing his "sorrow" that the priest had "fallen out with the spiritual world" and that he couldn't see that his angels were "those of Michelangelo, Raphael and the antiques and the best living models".

He wrote, "I know the world is a world of imagination and vision. I see everything I paint in this world, but everybody does not see alike. To the eye of a miser, a guinea is far more beautiful than the sun, and a bag warmed with the use of money has more beautiful proportions than a vine filled with grapes. The tree which moves some to tears of joy is in the eyes of others only a green thing which stands in the way. Some see nature all ridicule and deformity, and by these I shall not regulate my proportions, and some scarce see nature at all, but to the eyes of the man of imagination, nature is imagination itself. As a man is, so he sees. As the eye is formed, such are its powers. You certainly mistake what you say when you say that the visions of fancy are not to be found in this world. To me this world is all one continued vision of fancy and imagination." This is pure fire. And you can see why fire needs to be controlled, for unless it has a place in one's life, a place for expression, it loses touch with time and space reality, and goes mad.

Then he says, "What is it that set Homer, Virgil and Milton so high a rank of art? Why is the Bible more entertaining and instructive than any other book? It is not because they are addressed to the imagination, which is spiritual sensation, but immediately to the understanding or the reason. Such is true painting, and such alone was valued by the Greeks and the best modern artists." I think this is worth thinking about, as it says something profound about fire.

Fire is destructive unless it is controlled in some way. Fiery planets are moved by imagination, which he is calling spiritual sensation. I like that description of Mars conjunct Neptune in Leo in the 2nd house. Through Aries it acts. Through Leo it experiences itself intensely. Through Sagittarius it reaches for meaning, for understanding. As a Sagittarian with his Sun conjunct Jupiter, Blake reached through appearances into understanding and reason, and with his Leo emphasis he did it through art and through his way of life. And remember, what he means by "reason" is not what your ordinary two-dimensional mind is meaning. He is talking about Reason and Understanding as a fiery mind, a visionary mind.

Audience: His art controlled his fire?

Darby: His art both expressed and controlled his fire. Astrological fire has to be expressed. Planets in fire burn you up. They act creatively or destructively. If you live in the realms of the imaginal, if visions are part of your life, then generally you have to do something to bring them into being. Acquiring skills that can express the images creatively gives voice to the world of spirit. Listen to this:

> Tyger! Tyger! burning bright,
> In the forest of the night;
> What immortal hand or eye.
> Could frame thy fearful symmetry?
>
> In what distant deeps or skies.
> Burnt the fire of thine eyes?
> On what wings dare he aspire?
> What the hand, dare seize the fire?
>
> And what shoulder and what art,
> Could twist the sinews of thy heart?
> And when thy heart began to beat.
> What dread hand? & what dread feet?
>
> What the hammer? What the chain,
> In what furnace was thy brain?
> What the anvil? What dread grasp.
> Dare its deadly terrors grasp?

When the stars threw down their spears
And water'd heaven with their tears;
Did he smile his work to see?
Did he who made the Lamb make thee?

Tyger Tyger burning bright,
In the forest of the night:
What immortal hand or eye,
Dare frame thy fearful symmetry.

William Blake knew something about the act of creation. Sometimes it is as if he is there, in the very heart of it.

Both Blake and Himmler knew that what we see through the eyes of imagination is real. Their fire connected them to the world beyond the boundaries of our five senses. They knew that world as a "real world", and they each translated the images that burned through them in different ways. Himmler didn't think that astrology was dangerous because it was untrue. He thought it was dangerous because the astrologers might see something that didn't support the Nazi vision. William Blake, on the other hand, was furious at the people he felt had no vision, or whom he felt had chosen to operate from considerations other than spiritual sight.

The similarity between these two people is that they saw visions that moved them, and they believed their visions would be justified in the future. Himmler used power to try to express his vision. Blake used art to express his.

MORE ON SAGITTARIUS

Personal planets in Sagittarius

We have spoken about planets in Sagittarius through these two charts, and I would like to recapture some of the central images here. Those with **Sun in Sagittarius** shine their light on patterns of meaning. They often have a mission, though it might not be stated as such. They are lit up from within by what they see as real and true and, one way or another, they want to convince you that if you see what they do, the world will be a better place! Their vision is not personal; they are not necessarily seeing themselves at the centre. They are seeing something that they sense will make life better for them and theirs.

Their Jupiter placement will tell you more about where their vision is aiming. For instance, if Jupiter is in earth, then they are probably practical in getting their vision infused into their world. Blake has Sun conjunct Jupiter in Sagittarius, and he was primarily imaginative in expressing his vision. A Sagittarian with Jupiter in water might convey their vision so emotionally that it is only received by those who feel in sympathy with them, but it is none the less powerfully informing for all that. And I suddenly think of Edith Piaf, a Sagittarian with Jupiter in Pisces, who could break your heart with her songs of love.

A Sagittarian with Jupiter in air has all the ways of communication and interaction to speak through, and so generally it is easy to express the vision of his or her heart. However, the imagination needs the density of earth to shape it into something practical or something to be practised. It needs the intensity of water to bring soul experience to it and, therefore, to make it more loving or humane. It seems that vision has to be worked through the elements – although they may not easily receive it – to fulfil its purpose. Words and concepts and ideals are a natural conduit for the fire that informs each of us, but it still needs some immersion in water or earth to have an impact on its environment. Of course, this immersion can come through having a good proportion of the planets in water or earth houses. A Sagittarian with Jupiter in Gemini will find the words; a Sagittarian with Jupiter in Libra will find the elegant constructions; and a Sagittarian with Jupiter in Aquarius will find the right ideals to voice their truth. The real work is then to live their life, day to day, water and earth, according to these ideas.

Audience: Would that also be true for Sagittarius rising? I ask because I am Sagittarius rising, and I have Jupiter in Libra. I find life difficult emotionally and materially. I seem to live best in my mind, but I was blaming other things in my chart for that!

Darby: Well, the emotional and material difficulty may be shown by configurations in the water and earth domains. But I would think that having Sagittarius rising with Jupiter in Libra would make the life of the mind the natural way to journey through this life. You would have such a perfect sense of proportion, in some ways. And you would see where the proportion was wrong so quickly. Of course, it is off-centre almost everywhere except in certain "still points" of the mind. It could seem as though everything that wasn't simple and graceful and elegant was wrong. You can project that "wrongness" onto yourself or others or the world. Somewhere I think there is work to be done in the earth and water worlds, if that is the case.

When Jupiter is in fire and the Sun is in fire, well, then you can imagine that the imagination is fired with infinite potential for doing (Aries), being (Leo) or knowing (Sagittarius). Whether these images get expressed artistically or religiously, or through attending to cultural development, will depend on other elements in the chart.

With any planet in Sagittarius, look to Jupiter to see what image is burning there. If **Venus is in Sagittarius**, with her wild generousity and romanticism, her "high moral ground" and her passion for romantic adventure, look to Jupiter to see what vision fuels or impedes the heights and depths of her love nature.

Audience: I have Venus in Sagittarius in the 3rd, opposite Uranus in the 9th, and I have been quite reckless in my relationship life. But unless people know me very well, they would not suspect it. My Jupiter is in the 12th, and I guess that, when I compare myself to big-time romantic adventurers, I am pretty small-scale. But I have got into the canoe you spoke of before, and I might not have taken a first aid kit, but I did take my purse and my toothbrush! But I do have a good time when I'm having a good time, if you know what I mean!

The trouble is that I cannot imagine ever falling in love again, once I have been burned, and I become very critical of myself and others. But then something happens and I seem to get lit up again. I have a friend who has Venus in Sagittarius conjunct Jupiter. Now, that is big-time romance! She falls in love with men who invite her on round-the-world trips even now, at sixty-five! And once, on the way to one of her romantic adventures, I asked her where her suitcase was, and she said, "Oh, I'll buy what I need when I get there." I think I compare all other so-called romantics to her.

Darby: I agree with you – that's pure fire. There is no thought or image of what "might go wrong", and therefore, although they get burned here and there, they are usually ready for the next adventure quite quickly. But remember, there are other kinds of romantics besides fire romantics. Think of your water romantics.

There may not be much adventuring there for love, but there are certainly layers and layers of loving that are never seen from outside, by others.

Audience: I have Venus conjunct **Mercury in Sagittarius** in the 7th, and my husband is fifteen years younger than me. We met ten years ago, when I went to buy tickets to Verona. He was busking outside the travel agency.

Darby: I think someone must write a book called *Sagittarian Tales: Believe it or Not.* I know a man with **Moon in Sagittarius** in the 6th, who met his wife in a unisex loo on holiday in France. They were both English and a bit embarrassed, but then she made a joke and he fell in love. In general, Moon in Sagittarius comes across as being "in the know", and most of them are extremely funny. Jupiter will tell you where they are most likely to become wise and knowledgeable, after some mad adventuring and bad experiences. They are emotionally fired up by images that lead them to imagine huge possibilities, and all it takes is a willingness to struggle to bring the fruits of their imagination into "the real world". They figure life out pretty quickly, and they seem to have a guardian angel, which is just as well, as they take some surprising chances from day to day. The willingness to struggle can come from awkward juxtapositions of aspects or elements, or planets in houses that are not comfortable. But there has to be some will to put up with the struggle that accompanies fire's emergence into ordinary day-to-day life.

Audience: So with **Jupiter in Sagittarius**, the images are right there burning through you, and you believe passionately in what you see as the truth. But with **Saturn in Sagittarius**, there is no burning conviction, and yet people with this position seem very intense about their beliefs. Would you say that the image which fuels their convictions reside somewhere else?

Darby: Yes, you've got it. Saturn in Sagittarius will tend to take its spiritual authority quite seriously. It develops its philosophy out of its own personal experience, and that is probably why it takes itself so seriously. Jupiter will tell the other half of the story. By that I mean it will either fuel or mitigate this tendency. It seems as if there is a message written in lead in the fire of Saturn in Sagittarius: Learn Well. And so it does work hard to "get it right".

Saturn in Sagittarius people are working to develop confidence in their own beliefs, and they will express this development according to their Jupiter. If Jupiter is in Pisces, it will be quiet or subtle in its expression, or only express its convictions in certain circumstances. If Jupiter is in Aries, then it will express its beliefs passionately and perhaps even aggressively. We are always defensive where our Saturn is, and when it is in Sagittarius, that defensiveness will be described through Jupiter.

Outer planets in Sagittarius

I am not going to go through all of the planets in Sagittarius, because I want to say just a small thing about **Pluto in Sagittarius**. We've got it for some time now. Pay attention! If we keep awake to it, we are then part of its story. If you notice, Pluto went into Sagittarius when Jupiter was in Sagittarius too, and it will finally leave in 2008, when Jupiter is in Capricorn. So we will experience an entire Jupiter cycle within the time period of Pluto in Sagittarius. Every person alive will have a Jupiter return during this period – every person alive will experience Jupiter transiting through his or her whole chart. Interesting, yes? So, notice where it began, and keep tabs on the development of the relationship between your inner moral stance and your community and cultural relationships.

Over the years you should see yourself more able to imagine a wider world, a wider reality. Watch Jupiter as it transits whatever house or houses are ruled by Sagittarius. Keep an eye on what is being refashioned for the future. At least aim for greater wisdom and compassion as your cultural images, beliefs and philosophies – Pluto in Sagittarius – collapse and reform themselves. Don't get stuck on what happens to you. Attend your potential for reaching beyond the boundaries of your imagination, according to the matters of that house.

Keep alive the possibility that, when Pluto leaves Sagittarius, you will be better fitted for life on this planet because you have been educated by Jupiter in every sign and every house of the zodiac. You will have "walked a mile" in all sorts of different moccasins – your inner capacity for understanding will be so great that you can encompass the world. Well, keep the vision alive – but don't be disappointed if you don't reach it. Remember, fire is the realm where we reach for the stars, where all possibilities swirl and stream. The higher you reach, the further you generally get.

Audience: But Pluto in Sagittarius is also about dogmatism, the destruction of education, travel, the rise of fanatical visionaries who burn others for their beliefs...

Audience: Or about the transformation of education, and the way we see ourselves in relation to each other, countries, nations, religions...

Darby: Well, we can all speculate on what it is about, and some of us will get some of it with great accuracy, and most of us will miss what later seem to have been the important bits. But, as you know, I am more interested in the navigation of the journey through time rather than predicting the specific events along the way. We all have a sense of the things that are being targeted by Pluto in Sagittarius, and all of us will be involved in one way or another, as Pluto will transit every chart and what it sets off will touch every life. We are all implicated in the imagining of our collective future. Pay attention to the images that circle round your inner landscape. You may not be responsible for the images that arise, but you are responsible for how you attend and nurture them. End of sermon.

Audience: You were talking about Pluto in Sagittarius, and I realised that it is about to begin having its effect on the **Neptune in Sagittarius** generation. Pluto will be conjuncting their Neptunes over the next twelve years. I remember that as a very profound time of my life. I began studying astrology then. I have an idea you get connected to the world – your life – around the time of that conjunction. Of course, it also occurs around the time of the Saturn return for people around now. What do you think?

Darby: I wanted to discuss Neptune in Sagittarius. It has to be seen alongside its companion, Pluto in Libra. We are having such a long time of Pluto sextile Neptune; it will be very strange for us when they separate. They have been sextile since around 1930, and they won't part company until somewhere around 2020. The field that is undergoing change and transformation, at any time, is alongside that which is longed for, having been lost. I am playing with a sort of formula here, to get us thinking about Pluto and Neptune.

Pluto in Libra describes a time in which there was an underlying fear that peace would be lost, and that injustice would triumph. I am just putting the words together here, Pluto in Libra. Relationships between partners, whether personal or national, all fall into Pluto in Libra's realm, and undergo some sort of examining and transforming. Good relationships seem generally impossible without some sort of deep cleansing of ideas about relationship in general. Something has to change, and this is the group which is thrown into the caldron so that it may be changed through them.

Those with Neptune in Sagittarius dream of freedom, adventure, exploits. They are truly a dreaming generation, and they will adventure, or dream of it, way into old age. They carry some sort of wild faith in the future – and they also carry illusions which will come up against other realities as they go along. Some of them will journey far into inner and outer places that we cannot imagine yet. Through their adventures and discoveries, they will change the way we relate to each other. They will explore new realms and break through to new laws governing all sorts of relationships. They will break chains that we don't even know we have around us. Others will dream their lives away, chasing ecstatic experiences and avoiding any sort of true commitment, because of fear of what they might have to go through when they renounce their image of freedom (Neptune in Sagittarius) and when they make contracts with each other (Pluto in Libra). And they might be "contract junkies" too, thinking that is the illusory path to freedom.

I am fascinated by their art and music, though much of it does not speak to me, as the music of my generation did. But I imagine, when time sifts it out a bit, some strange and wonderful designs will appear which will give hints about the new patterns emerging. I am sure there are people who can see these patterns very clearly already. And what about education and air travel? Will they renovate education out of their disillusionment, and will they be the generation that experiences totally new forms of travel? What will their religious longing produce? And those with Uranus in Sagittarius, too – what weird and amazing imaginative realms will they access, on their quest for new forms of truth and meaning?

I have a client whose son has Neptune in Sagittarius conjunct his Sun, and Pluto in Libra conjunct his Moon. He has Jupiter in Cancer in the 2nd. He is eighteen, and seems to have no ambition at all. He lies around all day watching TV, and is often depressed. He has moments when he expresses deep understanding and compassion, but the rest of the time, he is mostly silent. His father left when he was three. His mother brought up her children alone, working in the social services. She is very worried about her son. I look at those conjunctions and I can see why she is worried, but I also know that if he can hang in there and keep gathering experience over the next ten years, he will probably begin to live an unusual and rich life. Young people with their personal planets strongly aspecting outer planets often seem lost in their teenage and early adult years. They have to go through all sorts of trials to unpeel themselves from conventional reality. They have a sense they are "made for something", but it is often impossible to imagine what it is.

This young man has his Jupiter in the 2nd, and once, when I asked him what he wanted, he said, "To be very rich, so I can travel anywhere I want whenever I want." I thought, "Well, that's a start." But I am sure there is more to who he is than that. He has not had enough experience yet to be able to fashion a vision from the different sorts of people he needs to meet. Because the Sun-Neptune conjunction is in the 7th house, it is as if there are certain people it is his destiny to encounter. He goes a distance on his journey with them, and then he is alone again. Then there is another one. Some of them are just brief encounters, between stations so to speak, but each is part of the story that will mine his resources until he has a sense of his own possibilities and he gets in touch with his realisable vision.

Going back to your question: I, too, think that when Pluto transits natal Neptune, if there is going to be a marked spiritual destiny, then that is one of the more potent gates through which the notions and images can arrive. Someone or something will come along and set it off. Not everyone with Neptune in Sagittarius will have a personal vision which they will be compelled to express or share with others. But those whose imaginal life must be communicated, those who have to live according to the dictates of their vision, will often find themselves taken by it around that time.

For the rest of the generation, they will have some fairly far-out tastes in entertainment, and somewhat wild notions of what sort of future they are moving towards. And for all the generation, the images they connect to will always be circumscribed by their individual Jupiter, of course. The young man I was just talking about sees his future in terms of money – Jupiter in the 2nd house. But he is the only son of a family of women, and has quite a kind and protective nature. I can imagine that he is envisioning himself as the future security of his mother and, if needs be, his sisters, with Jupiter in Cancer.

FIRE WITH OTHER ELEMENTS

Fiery people in earth-water generations

Audience: I have been noticing that sometimes people seem to be born into times that don't really suit them. For example, a very fiery person, with lots of personal planets in fire, might be born in 1965, and so have the Uranus-Pluto conjunction in Virgo opposition Saturn and Chiron in Pisces, and Neptune in Scorpio. That must be very frustrating.

Audience: But if you had it in you to make a mark, it would be quite a mark. Think of that generation born towards the end of last century, with Neptune, Chiron and Pluto in Taurus and Uranus in Virgo. Einstein, with all his personal fire – Moon in Sagittarius and Mercury, Venus and even Saturn in Aries, certainly made his mark. One of his troubles was that they turned his mathematical expression of the fire realm into something that was totally destructive on the physical plane.

Darby: Yes, I used to notice it with fiery people born in the late 1930's and early 1940's: Uranus in Taurus, Neptune in Virgo and Pluto in Cancer. You know how Pluto went between Cancer and Leo for years. These people incarnated into a time which was oppressed and dark and hard – where the values of their group have to do with security and stability, while they are personally wild, with images of adventure and deeds of daring. Well, they do stand out amongst their peers, don't they?

Audience: I just had a thought. My father is from that generation you are speaking of. I call it "the sensible generation". He always seemed to be one step ahead, and luckier than everyone else. He is Sagittarian, but with Neptune in Virgo, and he had both kinds of intuition. He is very sensible, with lots of earth, but takes chances because of his fire. He thinks he is down-to-earth and practical, because that is the way they like to think of themselves, but he is really taking quiet little leaps which are not earthy at all, but fiery. And they pay off.

Darby: Yes, there is a part of us that longs to be integrated into the community, no matter how much we protest against it. We want to fit in, and be absolutely unique at the same time. That's fair. It is dangerous not to fit in somewhere. I'll wager you that those with Neptune in Sagittarius, who adventure when they are young, will be the ones who are idealised when they are older. Others who just dreamed of it, or were too practical and so started doing practical things, will look at the dreamers who dared to go off and have their illusions exploded, and will consider they really did something worthwhile. Neptune becomes a sort of god to a generation. Jupiter may say something about what we worship personally, but Neptune is the unattainable and inaccessible beyond; and anyone we feel might have been there, or anywhere near there, and who comes back to tell the tale, becomes something of an icon in one way or another.

Audience: You had a few icons in your generation who went too far and "burnt out".

Darby: Yes, that is the difficulty when people live too close to the images that dominate a generation. Who are you thinking of?

Audience: Jimi Hendrix and Janis Joplin.

Darby: Does anyone know their charts?[1]

Audience: I do, because I am interested in musicians of the 1960's. They both had Moon and Jupiter in Cancer. Hendrix had them conjunct in the 7th house, and the Moon was close to Pluto in Leo in the 8th. He was a double Sagittarian with Mercury and Venus also in Sagittarius, in the 12th house – Mercury and Venus were in the 11th, but on the cusp of the 12th. Joplin didn't have the conjunction, but both Jupiter and the Moon were in the 5th house. She had Sun, Mercury and Venus in the 12th.

Darby: Both of them were very 12th house people, then. It is as if their urge to care for the deepest needs of others turned them into burnt offerings for the collective. Both with Moon and Jupiter in Cancer, too! So many musicians, composers and matinee idols of the 1930's and 1940's had Moon in Cancer. And such a private Moon too. And here, with all that 12th house! People with planets in the 12th really do have to take care with drugs and alcohol if they want to keep from being absorbed by the collective.

Audience: I wonder if that is true for all fiery people? I can image that alcohol is less troublesome if you have lots of earth to absorb it! I can imagine that water and fire people have to be more careful, because it fuels up the images.

Darby: And airy people?

---

1   For the reader's information, Jimi Hendrix was born on 27 November 1942, at 10.15 pm, in Seattle, Washington. Janis Joplin was born on 19 January 1943, at 9.45 am, in Port Arthur, Texas.

Audience: They're so rational that it can't be a problem for them. They decide how much is good to have and then do it.

Darby: That's interesting. I agree with you about the fiery people. I'd have to think about the others. But it is true that alcohol fuels imagination, and if your inner life is a riot of potentials and possibilities, then the alcohol will exaggerate them. But it might not help you then find the means to express them in such a way that you get satisfying results. But I hesitate to be judgemental here. There have been some amazing artists, writers, healers, actors, even cooks – all sorts of creative people who could channel their vision into something wonderful but could not control their drinking. Sometimes the gap between the vision and that which one creates from it is almost too hard to bear. Those who find a safe way to live with that gap are blessed indeed.

Singleton in fire

We have discussed an example of a fiery person in an earth-water generation. Let's imagine the opposite condition. What happens when the only planet you have in fire is transpersonal? All the other planets are in air, earth or water. Would you have anything to say about that?

Audience: Well, there are a lot of people around like that. I know several people whose only fire is Pluto in Leo. They are incredibly intense at times, but otherwise live rather quietly. There are three people I know with that. One is a Pisces with a Capricorn Moon, and she is normally quiet, but she has Pluto in Leo in the 3rd, and she can literally "burn your ear off" if she gets onto her obsession, and especially on the phone!

Audience: I know someone with Uranus in Leo in the 11th, and otherwise no fire – mostly earth and water, in fact. He works in a bank, but he belongs to this really strange club. They go away once a month and dress up in costumes and pretend to be a community of whomever they have decided to dress up as. They rent a house in the country and go off and be Martians, or the men pretend to be women and the women pretend to be men for the weekend. They experiment with all sorts of things.

Audience: I have an uncle with Uranus in Aries, and everything else in air and water. He is as mild as can be, and a very sweet man. However, if you ever talk about art, he turns into a wild man! He has Mars in Libra and he is very sure of his taste, which is pretty good, I must say. But he has these aberrations, and suddenly gets inspired, and rushes off and buys something so unexpected and – well, I have to say it – so strange. My aunt says he has always had this streak of unpredictability in him. It wouldn't be a problem at all, except that he spends huge amounts of money on these art objects, and then one day they simply disappear, and if you mention them he gets very angry.

Darby: And this probably keeps him the very nice man he is, the rest of the time.

Audience: My daughter is a Pisces, with Neptune in Sagittarius and no other fire. The only time I ever see her enthusiastic is when she is going off somewhere. Otherwise she has no idea what to do with her life. She drifts around in a dream, even though she is twenty already. I despair of her. Two years ago she went off alone to Australia. She didn't even have friends there. I was terrified, but I let her go because it was so wonderful to see her excited. She had a wonderful time. And she has been drifting around ever since, dreaming about her next trip. Do you think she will be like that for the rest of her life?

Darby: I don't think I could say from just that information, but give her time. I think you were wonderfully wise to support her going off so far away. It must have been very frightening.

Audience: It was. But I have several fiery planets, and I adventured a lot in my youth, so I am not plagued with imaginings of what horrible things might happen. I went all over the world on my own and mostly had a grand time. I did ask her to let me choose a good day for the start of her trip, and she liked that idea. Her next trip will be to India, but it is taking her a long time to get the money together.

Darby: I wonder if the outriders of this generation will go on pilgrimages of one kind or another.

Audience: Will they go to the Moon?

Audience: Some of them will go to the Moon, and the rest will dream about it.

Lack of fire

Audience: I've heard it said that if you don't have fire, you lack vitality. You lack enthusiasm. Well, I have no fire, and I seem more fiery to other people than my husband, who has one planet in fire.

Darby: Let's speak about this now. When there are no planets in an element, then you do not operate from the motivating power of that element. If there are no planets in fire, you are not pulled forward by visions of potential spiritual or creative fulfillment in the future. You do not see yourself as the central figure in the drama of life. You may be self-absorbed in another way, but not in the middle of a stage somewhere in your inner life. You are not driven by the search for meaning, or passionate about expanding the boundaries of the mental or physical world around you.

But you will attract people who are filled with enthusiasm for the unfolding of the future, and who are imagining life as they go along. If you lack an element, you attract it either in the people or the events of your life. Then you have to watch out that you don't get burned up in their vision of what is happening. Fire consumes, and your energy can be consumed by fiery people if you don't take care and attend. And while it is being consumed, you can think they are to blame because they are not taking you into account. So you sit on them or throw water on them or blow them away with all your words. And then you have lost the warmth and the heat. And they have lost the elements you brought to them, through which they could cook or shape or realise the vision that runs through them.

Audience: It is hard being around people with an element you are missing, but the other way round is uncomfortable too. I have noticed that people with no planets in earth will suddenly get obsessed with doing things absolutely right, and if you are around them while they are doing that, it is really boring. And when you are with non-watery people and they suddenly get emotional, it bursts out, and is very intense and obsessive, and then it is over. But they can go on and on and on analysing emotions for hours.

Audience: A missing element becomes an obsession.

Darby: Yes, it can. Those with no fire get all fired up by those who have fire. Those with no water become sloppy over watery people. With a missing element, just keep an eye on whether you are feeding off your fiery lover or friend and then disliking them for the very thing they are.

Audience: What about when there are no planets in fire, but a fire Ascendant?

Darby: Like Joan of Arc – Sun conjunct Venus in Capricorn in the 6th house and Leo rising. She had no planets in fire signs, and only one planet in a fire house, Mercury in Capricorn in the 5th. Jupiter is on the cusp of the 4th house, conjunct Moon in Libra in the 3rd. Yes, what about her! She heard voices and was directed by those voices in a very practical way. She has one planet in water, Neptune in Cancer, and the rest is earth and air. Isn't that interesting, with no fire? I only found her chart the other night when I had been playing with fire for a while. If any of you want to look at her chart, she was born on the 15th of January, 1412, in Domrémy, France and, the coordinates are 46N26 and 5E40. I have here 17:11 UT for the time.

Now, she was absolutely certain of her voices, with Jupiter conjunct her Moon in the 3rd. She found her meaning through her voices, and she looked like a fire visionary with Leo rising. She has a reputation as a visionary with Aries on the MC. But was she moving from a fiery vision? Or was she simply responding to the voices that she heard, which directed her to serve her king in that particular way? I think that she was responding to the call of her one water planet – Neptune in Cancer in the 11th house. She felt the collective longing through her one powerful water planet. She did not have a vision that drew her forward into a possible new world – she heard the cry of the collective and responded with all her practical intelligence.

Audience: But she actually "saw" various saints. That's visionary.

Darby: Well, we have to assume there are different sorts of visionaries. She did have Mercury in the 5th house, in Capricorn, and so she was able to see the saints who directed her, but she had no planets in fire signs.

Planets in fire move from conscious or unconscious images of something potential being actualised. Her images did not rise from that realm. In some ways, lack of fire is lack of imagination. She appeared to be immensely brave – she was not troubled by visions of torment or torture, except for once, near the very end. But she had overcome her fear by the next day. She heard voices and followed them and did what she had to do.

But there is an interesting fire connection. She began hearing voices around the time that transiting Neptune was conjunct her Ascendant. Did this activate a dream of glory in that Leo ascendant? Have you noticed the Neptune in Leo generation of our time, and their love of various notions of "glamour"? She had no planets in fire, but a fire Ascendant, and Neptune moved from Cancer to Leo around her thirteenth year. When you have a fiery Ascendant, and a planet in fire goes over it, then perhaps you will be lit up by images of whatever potential resides in that planet.

Audience: Neptune went over her Ascendant in Leo, and in her case she became a martyr and has had glory since her death. You were saying before that if you have no fire, you would attract fiery people to you. Well, in her case it was ridiculous – we don't know if she attracted fiery people to her, but she certainly attracted a fire!

Darby: Yes, she certainly did. Not even her progressed planets were in fire when she was burned at the stake – her progressed Moon was in Cancer, in fact.

Audience: Do you know that on the day of the great fire of London, there were no planets in fire in the chart? That's another instance of no fire attracting fire.

Audience: The baker in Pudding Lane said, "Let's put a bit of fire in this chart."

Darby: There was a little astrologer in Pudding Lane who was bored. He saw there was no fire, had his progressed Moon in fire, and thought, "What the hell."

Audience: My husband has only one planet in fire. He struggles with existential questions far more than I do, with no fire at all.

Darby: Is that true for you with no planets in fire? You don't struggle with the existential meaning of life?

Audience: Yes, I think it is true. I struggle more with what is there at hand. But I know a few people with no fire except Pluto in Leo. They don't struggle with meaning either, but they do lose heart at times, and you can then see that they were caught in some whirlpool, even if they didn't try to sort it out philosophically at the time.

Darby: Perhaps they were being "caught" by the image of transformation. "When the world/ I/it is different, then I will become my true self." We were speaking of having on Pluto in fire before. A client with Pluto in Leo and no other fire once said that he had noticed himself running that theme for years. He was at his Pluto-Pluto square, and he suddenly questioned his underlying assumption. It is this thing about people with only one planet in fire seeming more intensely fiery than those with lots of planets in fire. Whenever there is one planet in an element, it gets worked hard! One planet in fire, and when this person gets inspired, O Lord! do they leap into flame! And they have all those planets in the other elements through which to express themselves.

Audience: What happens to someone who doesn't have any fire when a reborn Christian comes up to him in the street and says, "Have you got Jesus?"

Darby: I don't know. Is this a riddle or a joke? What happens?

Audience: I don't know either, I was just wondering.

Audience: I have no fire, and I had that happen. One of them lost their faith on the spot, or so it seemed. I had two Jehovah's witnesses come to knock on my door, and when they left one of them was no longer a Jehovah's witness.

Darby: You put his fire out.

Audience: I did. It was very funny.

Darby: Not for him, it wasn't!

Audience: I have heard it is harder for people with lots of fire to manifest their spirit. Does that make sense?

Darby: I don't quite know what that means, but if you have several planets in fire, it can be so easy to live completely in your inner world. It takes challenging aspects with other elements to get the fire, the spirit, the images that arise in the inner world, into the outer world. The difficulty with lots of fire is that so much of your nature is connected to the imaginal plane, and when you try to bring some of that down into your material, emotional, or even your mental life, some of the shine goes off the original image. Saying this more simply: Things are seldom as perfect as we envision them. Imagine the book you will write, or the play, or the poem. Imagine how you would run the school, or the business or the government! Imagine how you will love, when the right person comes along! For the images to become creative, for the spirit to live, it seems to need the marriage with air and earth and water. And although the other elements demand a sacrifice of the purity of the images in the flame, once you dare to commit yourself to action, inspired by images, you are in service to life, and life gives back to you in kind.

Audience: What about people who have no planets in fire, but a strong Mars or Sun or Jupiter?

Darby: I can think of one author I have read with no planets in fire, and Sun conjunct Jupiter in Virgo. Classically, Jupiter in Virgo is not a "strong" Jupiter, but the Sun conjunct it makes it central to his chart. He wasn't burned at the stake, but he got a lot of "heat" from society because of his work. Do you know who I am talking about?

Audience: I think we need a bit more information here!

Darby: It's D.H. Lawrence. I can't say much about him now, as I don't have his whole chart in my head at the moment, but I do remember when I was reading him that I was struck by his lack of fire. I love his poetry. He goes so close to what he writes about. He does not give the impression that he is searching for the essence hidden behind the appearance. He looks straight at what he is seeing, if that makes sense. He has an extraordinary particularity. He had Mercury in Virgo, too, if I remember correctly. It is said he had very little faith in himself as a writer. A strong Jupiter, or a focal Jupiter, will expand the range of what it touches. It may bring restlessness and adventure, but not the passionate belief that fire brings. When one is "doing" one's Jupiter, one is wholly present in the act that is in accordance with the sign it is in. But it is simply not fiery!

Fire healers

Audience: When you did the water seminar you mentioned "water healers". Is there such a thing as fire healers?

Darby: Interesting. I immediately think of fire walking. We were talking about it during the break. Those who have done it are very inspired about it. I wonder if it is a cure for flagging imagination or flagging courage? But this is something else. Fire healers can breathe life back into you when have lost your energy or enthusiasm for life, or when your life no longer feels meaningful. They can see potential in you, and see it so clearly that you begin to see it too. The negative side of fire healers will operate when their light beams so bright that your own light seems smaller. They can be so sure of their own vision that if you don't follow their way, they lose interest in you.

Aries healers can galvanise you into action, but can also lose interest in you before you want them to. The solar healer can inspire you with the wonder of your own life and its undreamed-of possibilities, but they can also show off their own splendour in such a way that you lose heart. And the Sagittarian healer can weave the pieces of your life together so beautifully that it all begins to make sense again. But they can be blind to patterns of meaning alien to their own, and leave you feeling less wise and intelligent than they seem to be. It all depends on whether other things in the chart of fiery healers constellate humility and compassion. Fire is not compassionate unless it is tempered by other elements. When we identify too strongly with the fiery side of ourselves, we identify with the infinite potential that sits at the heart of all creation. That gives rise to impatience, not compassion. It is only after living a long time with our fire selves, and experiencing the difficulties of bringing vision into manifestation, that we begin to feel compassion.

Fire with other elements

Audience: Is fire better with air than earth or water?

Darby: Fire needs oxygen to live. It needs air if it is to be translated into words, ideas, concepts and structures that can be discussed and worked with. Do you know that T.S. Eliot has a chart that is all air and fire, and no earth or water? We'll look at his chart together one day. Being a poet was the most perfect way for him to satisfy that heavily unbalanced chart.

When a chart is dominated by two elements, you usually find that the person finds a particular field in which to operate. Then they just stay there – they don't waste time with the other sides of life. Charts that are predominantly fire and earth are often very effective charts. Of course, there are those who just go back and forth between the world of imagination and the mundane world, and that must be very unsatisfying and lead to a kind of boring arrogance.

But most of the people I have met with that combination turn their visions into buildings, gardens, books, statues and paintings. It is not an easy or comfortable combination at all – they get ravaged by the effort of their tasks. Think of a blowtorch fashioning a piece of sculpture out of metal, by a master hand! These people get better and better at turning their images into things that serve life.

Audience: My chart is all water and fire. Completely useless, I always think.

Darby: Except at loving, tending, caring, inspiring, feeling and being wholly alive.

Audience: Oh, I don't know...

Darby: Fire and water is all feeling and passion. Images rise from the past and the future, and weave a complex emotional story. In my early days as an astrologer, we would have said something like, "Your life is about the development of your soul and spirit, and everything else is irrelevant." And that may be the best way of saying it. A chart full of fire and water is all about the day-to-day living with oneself and others, their memories and imagination, your memory and imagination, the interweaving of the two. Fire and water live out the "whole catastrophe", as they say.

We are at the end of the day, and there is a poem by a Persian poet of the fourteenth century that I would like to read to you. I love his poetry because it is so religious, and so utterly different to my own tradition. Like other poets of his tradition, he conceives of God as "the lover", "the friend", "the beautiful rascal", and so on. The poet is called Hafiz – Shams-ud-din Muhammad Hafiz. I am reading it from *The Subject Tonight is Love,* which contains many of his poems. It is called, "We Keep Each Other Happy and Warm".

> Like two lovers who have become lost
> In a winter blizzard
> And find a cozy empty hut
> In the forest,
> I now huddle everywhere
> With the Friend.
> God and I have built an immense fire
> Together.
> We keep each other happy
> And warm.

Okay, thank you for an exciting day. Keep warm!

BIBLIOGRAPHY

Blake, William, *Songs of Innocence and of Experience,* Tate Gallery Publications, London, 1991.

Corbin, Henry, *Temple and Contemplation,* Islamic Publications, London, 1986.

Raine, Kathleen, *William Blake,* Thames and Hudson, London, 1970.

Ravenscroft, Trevor, *The Spear of Destiny*, Samuel Weiser Inc, NY, 1971.

Picture credits: Photo of Himmler from Gerald Reitlinger, *The SS,* Heinemann, 1956. Portrait of Blake by John Linnell, pencil, 1820, Fitzwilliam Museum, Cambridge.

ABOUT THE AUTHOR

Darby Costello took a degree in psychology, philosophy and theology in New York and then studied astrology in Boston in the 1960s. From there she went to Africa, where she was part of a small team in the Museum of Man and Science in Johannesburg, recording and transcribing the sacred lore of tribal healers and diviners for posterity.

She has lived in London since the early 1980s. Since 1988 she has taught and written books for the Centre for Psychological Astrology, founded by Liz Greene and Howard Sasportas in 1983. Her first book, *Astrology,* was written with Lindsay Rademacher and published in 1996 by Dorling Kindersley for their Pocket Book series. That same year, *The Astrological Moon* was published by the newly created CPA Press. That was followed by *Water and Fire* (1998) and *Earth and Air* (1999). Darby was a contributor to *The Mars Quartet* (2001), along with Liz Greene, Melanie Reinhart, and Lynn Bell. She has contributed articles for various astrological publications in England, Europe, and America.

Darby is a tutor for the Faculty of Astrological Studies in London and a visiting tutor for the London School of Astrology. She teaches and lectures throughout Europe, and has taught in far-flung places such as Bali, and in many parts of North America, including Fairbanks, Alaska.

In 2006 Darby was awarded an MA in Cultural Astronomy and Astrology by Bath Spa University. This has given her a greater taste for history and a deeper love of writing. She received the Charles Harvey Award for Exceptional Service to Astrology in

2013. After all these years and experiences, her first love as an astrologer is still doing charts for people, and her worldwide clientele is the ground out of which her astrological inspiration is nourished.